Gray Faith

Carrye Burr

Copyright © 2016 Carrye Burr

All rights reserved. All rights reserved. No portion of this book may be reproduced, stored in a retrieval system, or transmitted in any form or by any means- electronic, mechanical, photocopy, recording, scanning, or other- except for brief quotations in critical reviews or articles, without the prior written permission of the author.

Cover design by Jeffrey Burr

All Scripture quotations, unless otherwise indicated, are taken from the Holy Bible, New International Version®, NIV®. Copyright ©1973, 1978, 1984, 2011 by Biblica, Inc.™ Used by permission of Zondervan. All rights reserved worldwide. www.zondervan.com The "NIV" and "New International Version" are trademarks registered in the United States Patent and Trademark Office by Biblica, Inc.™

ISBN-13: 978-0692744710
ISBN-10: 0692744711

ACKNOWLEDGMENTS

To my husband, Jeff- thanks for supporting me the whole way, helping me see a vision of what could be, and for your gift of cover art! I love you!

To the very first "Gray Faith" study group, thank you for your encouragement and willingness to help. You gave me a new passion to see the stories and discussion that can only flow through honesty.

To Carlee, thanks for essentially being my editor, and never giving up on me. You helped make this what it is.

To Kim, thanks for mentoring me and lending a plan to my scattered dream.

To my parents, thank you for lovingly believing in my dream of writing, and for raising me to find gray faith for myself.

CONTENTS

	Introduction	vii
1	Gray Beginnings	1
2	Gray Christian Culture	17
3	Gray Church	29
4	Gray Sin	43
5	Gray Evangelism	53
6	Gray Expectations	65
7	Gray Walk	77
8	Gray Answers	91
	Study Guide	105
	Notes	123
	About the Author	127

INTRODUCTION

HELLO, I'M A PK

Some things in life follow you around the way the scent of someone else's perfume follows you after you hug them. It might not be something you chose for yourself, but it envelops you anyway. My hand-me-down scent was being a pastor's kid (PK). It's humorous when people see you in a certain light based solely upon what your parent does for a living. Once in high school I said something (borderline) inappropriate, and my friend quipped, "Hey, you can't say that! You're a PK!"

Really, I didn't mind being a pastor's kid- I was actually proud to be. My childhood may have been "different", but I feel genuinely privileged to have been raised in a family that seemed to defy the norm. Whatever that is.

That said, it wasn't always easy. When I was just a few years old my parents chose to actively live out their faith by moving from the south where I was born to a tiny town in Massachusetts. Since then we've moved states three more times in the pursuit of following God's direction. I've experienced public, private, and homeschooling, and I've felt the pressure of ministry and financial uncertainty that often came with a pastoring job. Though close with my family, I struggled for many years to develop long-term friendships.

But one of the most challenging things about growing up in a pastor's home, immersed in Christian culture, has been this fight to see faith for myself, from outside the Christian "bubble". It's so natural to believe what our parents teach us about spirituality. From that family platform it didn't occur to me to challenge the larger spiritual culture. But at some point we drift either to automatic faith that goes along with what we've always known, or we bump into questions and concerns that, once confronted, will change our faith forever.

Raising kids in a Christian culture can be a wonderful thing, but that culture isn't perfect and sometimes does more harm than good. Now that I have three kids of my own, I'm more in tune than ever to how Christian culture and my own parenting affect my kids on their spiritual journey.

THE GOOD, THE BAD, AND THE UGLY

By very nature I'm a critical person- I'd like to call it discernment, because that's a gift of the Spirit, and criticism isn't. Call it what you will, my natural questioning keeps me balanced. I want to see more than one side to everything, and I don't want to believe anything just because you tell me to.

I'm also an introspective writer, living inside my head for large chunks of time. I have mounds of journals dating back to before my teen years. They're not all great reads, of course- I was a teenage girl once, with painfully single-minded musings. But understanding myself over the years gives me insight into my soul journey towards faith. I can see pieces of my Christian upbringing that were beautiful and drew me to God, and other aspects that clouded my understanding of God or even pushed me farther from His heart.

What I've found is that sometimes the very answers we know so well keep us from really experiencing the God we claim to follow. Sometimes the message of Jesus feels a bit packaged and perfect and we replace the real Jesus for a plastic one that's supposed to make everything OK. And when we're so saturated with this message of Jesus but unable to experience the fullness of Him, we aren't really motivated to share Him with a world that needs what real Jesus can give.

This book is my attempt to pick through the bits and fragments of my Christian family and culture to find how they shaped my faith today. For better or worse. My life isn't remarkable- I won't rivet you with tales of near death experiences or of training pigeons to drop Gospel tracts on unsuspecting heads. But I hope that you'll see in my experience something of your own, whether you believe in God or not.

In America, at least, it's hard to imagine someone who hasn't been impacted in some way by that broad and ambiguous swath we call "Christianity". This book is shaped by questions, and I can't pretend to have answers to all of them. I also don't expect that everyone will have the same positive or negative reactions to elements of the church that I did. Whatever my negatives may have been, I still very much believe in God.

Being in the presence of Jesus has become a very precious and real thing in my life.

My desire is that those who read this book are willing to ask themselves some hard questions. In the appendix of the book you'll find study questions for self-reflection or for use within a small group. I encourage you to try them out! We can't move forward with our stories, with real faith of any kind, if we never stop to examine our lives and the reasons for our beliefs. I hope that somehow my observations from the inside of the church will help you sort out your own faith journey or at least your interactions with those of us who call ourselves Christians.

1
GRAY BEGINNINGS

GOOD CHRISTIANITY

"Good Christianity" lied to me. "Good Christianity" told me God was black and white. It told me that being a Christian was largely about morality- oh, and telling others about Jesus so they could be moral too, I guess- but mostly so we could all go to heaven. Because "good Christianity" told me that heaven was the goal: a safe place, a happy-ever-after, instead of a perpetual furnace of misery. No one wants that.

Somehow, woven into my childhood were so many strands of "good Christianity" that sometimes I couldn't see the real God for the man-made one. It didn't occur to me that the hardest parts of life, the most confusing and gray things, might actually be the very places I'd find a God bigger than my "good Christianity".

I cut my teeth on church, you see. My very first memory, at just three, is being in a church nursery getting a hair barrette from a church lady. (I feel like I should say "church" once more for good measure.) We lived down south, then, in the Bible Belt, near my Jesus-believing, ministry-soaked, extended family. The spiritual legacy passed down to me over generations is truly priceless; but sometimes when faith is an heirloom treasured by others, it takes a long time to understand the breadth of its significance for yourself. I knew early on that God was supposed to be my everything, but He was hidden behind layers of religion, like dust and grime on beautiful mahogany.

Morality- being good- was the first layer of religion I had to dust off to understand God. The South I was born into is home to a plethora of churches, but also a healthy dose of legalism. For instance, the southern Christian college that my parents went to had strict rules about entertainment (no playing cards, people!), guys could get demerits if their hair was too long, and couples could only date with a chaperone. Sometimes the appearance of wrong was frowned on just as much as wrong itself.

Then there's my precious, godly, Memaw, who has only ever worn skirts and dresses. I don't think she saw ME in a pair of pants until I was nearly ten. My mom gradually allowed us to wear pants over time when we visited- as though perhaps no one would notice the change if it happened over several years. But my mom still insisted that we wear dresses to church for many years, a lingering vestige of rules and expectations that we dangerously intertwined with God Himself. Though meant to enforce God's heart, the rules often became a superficial indicator of spirituality. "Good Christianity" seemed to eclipse good God.

At age three, I moved away from the South with my family up to Massachusetts where my dad started a church out of our rented home. Church happened all around me on a weekly basis, and it was comfortable to me. God was comfortable to me, as though He were a well-worn plush toy I'd had since infancy. But even as my parents were shifting away from following the "good Christianity" of the South, I was picking up my own rules about Christianity that threatened my ability to truly encounter Jesus.

My parents set their own guidelines and rules for us based on what they believed God's heart was. There was a slew of TV shows, movies, books and more from pop culture that we weren't allowed to see or engage in. I remember not being able to watch *The Smurfs*, I presume because they promoted some suspicious element of magic. Or was it that you can't trust those noses? Hm. Later, we weren't allowed to read the *Harry Potter* books, because of the sorcery, and we cut up our *Pokémon* cards when we found out they were really "pocket monsters". (The horror!)

We also listened almost exclusively to Christian music, which to this day leaves me feeling like I've missed out on a normal cultural experience. Play a song by some obvious, well-known band like the Beatles or Bon Jovi and I'd have no clue; my wheelhouse was more like Sandi Patty and Steven Curtis Chapman.

Part of my rule-following was inherent in my compliant personality- I accepted most of what my parents said I shouldn't do and never felt the need to push boundaries too far. To this day, I still sometimes worry more about following the rules than the heart behind them. (Which reminds me, what age does my child have to be to disqualify me from parking in the "new mother" parking spot at the grocery store?)

Rule-following was a game I could play and win- that I could beat others at. Though God and His power and love were preached loudly enough, rule-following became the subtle goal of Christianity.

But if Christianity is reduced to morality, morality gradually overtakes our need for God. When we focus on following rules, we'll find that some are easy to follow. Turns out wearing dresses and saying nice things instead of "cuss words" and watching *Veggie Tales* instead of *Beevis and Butthead* isn't all that complicated. So we start to believe that God's role is making the rules, and our job is to obey them on our own.

Ironically, the more rules we think we can obey on our own- the less we need God. Moreover, we start to believe we can measure our own rightness with God against what we believe other people are failing at.

See, because I didn't question rules, I instead questioned those who broke them. The rules of my upbringing kept me from some unhealthy things, but they also made it easier for me to judge other people who acted outside my view of good. I struggled to see that godly people might enjoy Harry Potter without being sinful, or that, gee, maybe playing *Dungeons and Dragons* doesn't naturally lead to Satanism.

I also didn't understand that, while God's rules were meant for our good, we could never really fulfill them outside of His help. I knew the Bible said, "There is no one righteous, not even one"[1] and nod, *'yes, of course'*- but didn't I *feel* righteous deep in my heart, as though I was one of the few that verse didn't *really* apply to? Didn't I feel like I was as close to good as someone could be?

I had no idea how very, very small I'd made God and His love next to my mountain of worthless righteousness. I had no idea how much more of God hid under my layer of moral grime.

GRACE FOR THE OTHER BROTHER

I have this random memory of watching *I'll Be Home for Christmas* with my mom. (Come on, ladies, remember that one with Jonathan Taylor Thomas?) In one scene there's a girl who, desperate for a ride home, ends up driving with this guy she isn't crazy about. They have to stop overnight at some ridiculous winter-themed hotel and the last available room is a romantic suite with one bed. The girl allows the guy to sleep on the bed next to her, but makes him sleep on top of the covers to make her boundaries clear.

The "good Christian" in me knew that she shouldn't be sharing a bed with the guy even if no funny business happened. But I remember my mom applauding that moment in the movie- that the girl slept with the guy without "sleeping" with the guy. And this may sound crazy, but that moment roughly sums up the idea I had about grace.

I thought that grace always abounded for the person who didn't follow God. Whatever awful thing they might be doing was always forgivable the moment they turned to God. Gracious, we could even give them a gold star for doing things that were *almost* good. Bless their heart.

But as a Christian, once you crossed that initial line of grace, it sort of seemed like being good was an obligation. There was no room for "almost" good anymore. I think I lived as though grace gave me a great job that I really didn't deserve, but now I had to work my tail off to maintain that position. I grew up thinking that God cared an awful lot about whether I was "good".

But there's a parable in the Bible that breaks down what God really wants from us. It paints graceful strokes of God as a father, blending and adding dimension to the God who at other times is portrayed as stern, unapproachable and angry. The father in the story has two sons: one son decides long before his dad dies that he wants his share of the inheritance now. He takes off and squanders his wealth quickly, only to trade his luxury for a desperate poverty. He becomes so miserable that he regrets all his actions and decides to humbly return to his father, if only as a servant.

What he doesn't know is that his father has been waiting for him- looking for him every day. Because what the father really wants isn't a perfect son, but a son who *wants to be with him*. So while the son is still some distance away his father runs down the road to meet him. This gracious father not only accepts his son back into the home as though nothing had happened, but also throws him a giant welcome home party- no expense spared. This is the story of the loving God who waits for all of us, regardless of our past.[2]

But then there's the other son in the story- the son that represents me- that represents those of us who grew up with "good Christianity". This son knew better than to run away with his dad's money. He knew the house rules and he had been keeping them- religiously, you might say.

So when he hears what kind of welcome his dad is throwing for his delinquent brother, he's actually angry. Spitting mad. Truthfully, this is where I've sometimes checked out and told myself that I'm better than the other brother. Good grief! I can't imagine ever being angry about God welcoming someone else into the family. If someone ran up to me today saying, "Heeey!! I told God I just want to be with Him now, and He's doing awesome things for me!", my reaction would not be to seethe in anger and sulk away to keep from punching them in the nose. It's a no-brainer; I'd be genuinely happy.

But if I do a little character assessment I have to conclude that the self-righteous son still represents me. One of the most sobering moments in the parable is when the second son says:

"Look! All these years I've been slaving for you and never disobeyed your orders. Yet you never gave me even a young goat so I could celebrate with my friends."[3]

And the dad responds: *"you are always with me, and everything I have is yours."*[4]

It turns out the second son wants his inheritance too, or at least some extra blessings- but he has gotten everything all twisted. He's begun to believe that he has actually *earned* the right to his inheritance. He's stopped believing that the good things he ultimately receives are because of his relationship with his father, because of grace. Not only has he convinced himself that he somehow deserves his father's blessings, he's forgotten that the benefits of being with his father, of being a son, are always available to him and far outweigh his inheritance.

Does that sound like you at all? Because it's my story.

I turn into that brother when I start thinking maybe I'm just a little bit better than so-and-so, or that I'm certainly trying a lot harder. Sometimes I'm that brother when life gets hard and I bitterly throw questions at God, asking why I should bother sacrificing so much of my life for Him if he isn't going to fix everything or throw me a party. I turn into that brother when I forget that my need for God's grace doesn't end just because I'm in the family. God's mercy makes me His child when I don't deserve it, and it turns out that only in that same grace can I do anything meaningful in this life.

I've also been the second son when I forget that God's presence is the greatest grace of all. It turns out my idiot brother's mistakes made him humble enough to draw closer to that presence. Ironically, all my so-called "good deeds", when done in my own strength, actually drive me farther from my Father.

Is it possible that the real tragedy in the story of the prodigal son is not so much the prodigal, but the "good" son that never knew what it meant to be living daily in God's grace? Is it possible that we can't experience all of God until we unravel completely before Him and acknowledge how utterly incapable we are of keeping up this perfect Christian shtick?

When we choose to try righteousness on our own, we're actually striving for what grace already gave us.

I'm slowly dusting my religion off- I'm settling into a God who's more concerned with surrendered hearts than perfect morality. I'm learning that the grace that first drew me to Jesus, instead of leaving me to strive towards righteousness on my own, actually grows more precious as I know my Father more. I'm a long way off, but I desperately want to know what it looks like to walk in the grace of the Father's promise that everything He has is mine. Grace isn't just once for each of us, but new every morning.[5] What beautiful life can that awaken in me- in you?

AVOIDING ABRAHAM

So if morality wasn't the ultimate goal of Christianity, what was? I had grown up with all the facts about Jesus. I knew so well the stories and right answers and it all seemed to confirm that I was doing just fine. Fine but empty. Knowledge of the rules didn't equate to knowing God- knowing all the stories about other people in the Bible didn't give me a personal story with God.

Christianity is about God coming to be with us, to interact with us, to completely invade our lives in a marvelous but insane way. Morality is much safer and doesn't actually require that much faith, because morality is more or less about what *we* do. But to interact with God is to acknowledge *His* work in the midst of everything. When we expect God to show up in our lives, faith becomes less about following the rules, and more about following the Spirit...which doesn't feel safe or tidy.

The problem is, "good Christianity" doesn't like to rock the boat too much. Sometimes being a Christian seemed more like dressing up for a church service than showing up to experience a God who might actually want to be actively involved in our lives. I was so close to the stories that I often missed the fact that the same power, the same relational God from the Bible was ready to act in my life. Knowing God and articulating my faith (talk) was not the same as experiencing God in a tangible way (power).[5]

But my faith got a bit more real at a "family meeting" when I was ten years old.

My friends laugh about our family tradition of meetings, especially after watching *Arrested Development*. But it was one of our ways to bond and discuss our lives as a family, even if that occasionally meant hashing out chores. Often our family meetings merged into Bible conversations; we'd bring our notebooks and Bibles, feeling a bit important and businesslike, prepared to write down whatever spiritual or domestic tidbit applied to us.

That particular day, my dad called us out to our three-season porch and quickly launched into Genesis 12, the Bible story about Abraham. The guy is 75 years old and God basically says, *"I want you and your family to pack up your stuff and leave behind everything you've ever known."* And the kicker was there was no road map. There wasn't even a destination. God just said, *"Go...to the land I will show you."*[6] My siblings and I were probably writing things down as fast as we could, dutifully admiring Abraham's faith in an attentive but detached way.

Little did we know.

Next my dad made the Biblical application segue of a lifetime: He said that we, like Abraham, were moving to a place God would show us. Except Dad wasn't 75 years old, and he was decently sure we were moving to Alabama to help my uncle pastor a church there.

My dad went on to say that recently while he'd been lying around sick (something he almost never was), he began to sense God directing him to move. He shared how he and my mom then started praying about the move together and that God kept nudging them. Our family now jokes that if my dad gets sick or mentions Abraham we should get ready for a big change. So we kind of avoid Abraham.

But I still remember as they shared their hearts that I felt like I was on the inside of some divine adventure. I would eventually process more of the hard parts like leaving friends and our little home in Massachusetts, but I also had this expectancy, this sense that there was something thrilling in the unknown.

Looking back, that move was probably one of the single most life-altering pieces of my story. "Good Christianity" thrives in safety and routine, but the move instantly uprooted me from my comfort zone and broadened my narrow world. Because the move would happen mid-school year, my parents took the opportunity to start homeschooling us when I entered sixth grade, another gigantic change. Right in the middle of that awkward middle school year I was dropped into a place where I knew almost no-one and felt true insecurity for the first time.

But however hard, it was the best thing that could have happened to me. In fact, my parents' decision to follow God's heart all the way across the country probably did more for my faith than going to church every week my whole life. To hear a Bible story or book about a character's life altering faith is one thing- to watch my parents live it out was another. It was my parents' faith that moved us, yes- but they included us in their faith journey instead of sheltering us from the process.

This became a natural breeding ground for my own faith. And when it became clear years later how God used our family each time my parents responded to Him, I could also see the result of my parents' faithfulness- which gave further credibility in God for my own faith to stand on. It gave a greater sense that this Bible thing was not just a story to be read but one to be lived out.

We won't all move our children across the country. But in each of us is a God-given passion for something beyond ourselves, beyond our means to produce or create on our own. It's that desire inside you that people either think is completely crazy or hail you as a saint for.

The things we do that show our kids true faith are as varied and unique as we are. It could mean traveling to other countries; praying for years for a spouse or friend to see God; staying in a ministry or job for years to honor God when it would have been easier to quit; following a God-dream that requires giving up financial security; leaving family or making any change that is outside your comfort zone or your abilities in order to follow God. For my family, part of our ongoing "crazy" has been adoption (see chapter 7) and who knows what's next.

When I witnessed my parents' constant "crazy faith", it didn't seem so crazy after awhile- it became normal. And before I ever had to put faith in God all on my own, I got to watch how He showed up for my parents, for my family, for what we didn't have a map or resources for. So when it came time to step out in faith on my own- for finances, for medical issues- faith was in my DNA.

I'd seen faith at work when the stakes were lower for me personally, which helped me be confident that the God who wrote my parents' story would write mine too. I began to see that God is actually keenly interested in writing my story if I will let Him. Maybe following God was more about an adventure than getting through life mistake-free. The facade of "good Christianity" was cracking.

A BROKEN YEAR

The move of faith to Alabama turned out to be one in a series of moves. After just three eventful years in the Heart of Dixie, we moved back to our old town in Massachusetts. My dad picked up a job teaching at a small, private Christian school, so I spent ninth grade wearing pleated skirts and a tucked in polo shirt while trying to grow out an awkward haircut.

Even with just ten kids in my class, I experienced more traditional socialization and exposure to life outside my home than I'd had in the past three years of homeschool. I struggled to fit in, but eventually found myself passing little origami-folded notes to other girls, and even laughing over inside jokes. (Who knew I could have one?)

Our Christian school had its spiritual perks, like chapel and godly teachers, but it was hardly free from the influence of the world. I was a bit shocked to discover friends who smoked pot, for instance, or used language that I was quite certain no "good" Christian should use. I tried to wrap my mind around the inconsistencies I was seeing, which rammed full force into my wall of "good Christianity".

Unfortunately, by tenth grade the private school I attended closed for financial reasons. The excitement of watching my parents follow God waned as I watched my dad in a season of transition, between jobs and uncertain of the next step. I waited for my life to move forward as well as I returned to homeschool and my friendships dwindled.

Aside from occasional homeschool groups, there were a few kids in my neighborhood I'd see from time to time, but I didn't remotely know how to relate to them. Somehow the girl who walked by with a carton of cigarettes stuck down her shirt was so far from my "pure" world I felt brave just standing with her and the others. I couldn't manage a normal conversation for more than a few minutes with the skinny neighborhood boy with baggy pants and glasses. What should I talk about? For all I knew, I was probably just supposed to be sharing Jesus with him anyway, which didn't help the relational pressure.

The combination of multiple moves, constant school transition, and a frustrated desire to be liked by boys made me feel like something was wrong with me. So as a fifteen year old I remember almost a year of trying to eat as little as possible (as in a couple hundred calories per meal) and to run as often as I could. I was the skinniest I've ever been but still felt huge (not an uncommon teenage girl story). I don't think I knew what I wanted other than being wanted, and I suspect that I would have racked up a lot of regret if I'd actually gotten much attention from guys I liked at that time.

Though I loved the benefits of learning at home, that year I felt a strong sense of isolation and very real loneliness. At a time when teens are naturally questioning their parents and looking to peers to grow and shape them, I had little outlet for processing my struggles. Certainly this may have saved me from negatives of peer pressure, but it also kept me somewhat in the dark.

I lacked confidence in who I was and was extremely focused on what I didn't have relationally. Without a really tight network of friends, I got lost in myself and didn't know how to find my way out in a positive way.

I also remember verbally questioning faith with my parents in that season, finally putting Christianity itself under the microscope.

"Do I really believe this God stuff? What if I only buy into all this because I've grown up with it?"

I'm deeply grateful to both my parents for not panicking in response to my doubts. I remember an honest conversation with my dad about my faith uncertainty and if he was inwardly hurting or surprised he never showed it. In a way it was as though he gave unspoken permission for me to doubt,

and that permission to seek truth on my own in the gray of life did more good for me than any lecture, pleading, or panic would have done.
I share this part of my story to emphasize that Christianity doesn't protect us and our kids from the parts of the world that are broken. I believed in God, grew up largely sheltered from ideals of the world, and had two parents who loved and followed Christ in everyday life; but this did not save me from unhealthy views of myself, my body, my worth.

I'm human- I'm broken- and just like Eve who had only God for a Father, I'm susceptible to the lies of the enemy and the downward spiral that results when I act on those lies. To assume that we or our own kids won't struggle, fail, or fall out of faith at some point is unrealistic. Further, it sets us up for burdensome guilt and pressure.

Although watching my parents pack up and move to follow God was like oxygen for my faith, it didn't come without pain and loss for me. Gray parenting means stepping out in faith knowing that our kids will probably wrestle because of our choices. It means recognizing that there's no one right solution to schooling or parenting, just as there isn't a sure fire way to protect our kids from being bruised by the world or confronted with difficulties.

No matter what our parenting approach, we'll have to be proactive and diligent in helping our kids with issues of faith, socialization, loving the world and loving themselves. In the end, we can only offer them a gray childhood- a lot of love, mixed with some inevitable mistakes. We can aspire to live out a Christianity in our own lives that is more focused on interacting with God than in following rules. Scary or liberating, we don't get to control the choices our kids make and what they do with their own faith.

MISSING SOMETHING

Just as limitless grace undermines the lie of "good Christianity", so does humility. Two of the greatest gifts my parents gave me were their willingness to think critically about the applications of faith they had grown up with, and their ability to admit over time their own shortcomings and faulty beliefs.

My dad once shared with me that growing up he rarely heard messages at church about reaching out to the poor. There are whole chunks of scripture that he feels were downplayed at best, ignored at worst. Though he places the responsibility on himself, he said that when he first began pastoring he, too, largely overlooked the call of the Bible to reach out to the poor- to the "least of these".[7]

In more recent years, especially after traveling to the impoverished community of Jido, Ethiopia, he realizes how far he was from God's heart. I suppose the proof of his growth in this area is that he's currently serving in a missional pastor position, and I wouldn't be entirely surprised if one day he packed up the last three shirts he owns and moved to Ethiopia.

My dad has always loved God. Period. But he modeled for me that following God probably means that I SHOULD feel differently about some things in ten years than I do now, because that means I'm allowing God to grow me. The way I live now is based on my love and understanding of God now- but this side of heaven I will never arrive at perfection, I will always have room to grow closer to God's heart.

If I always have room to grow closer to God, am I ever really as good as I should be? Am I ever really free from the need for God to change me?

In my teen years I didn't always agree with my parents' decisions. (There's a shocker.) But I remember specifically both of my parents coming to me after different disagreements to acknowledge that I was right, or that they could see the validity in my side. They were humble enough admit that their own children might occasionally make a better decision or have a healthy insight they missed.

To grow up in an environment like that gave me confidence in seeking God in making my own decisions, even if it sometimes took me in a different direction than others thought best. It helped me see that humility and admission of wrong isn't weakness. Rather, assuming we're always right is weakness- weakness that perpetuates self-righteousness.

As a parent now myself, I know my kids will see me make mistakes or miss the mark in life. But I hope that through that, they see a mother who's still learning and being stretched. I hope that I'm not too proud and stubborn to let them see my journey towards allowing the Spirit change those parts of my thinking that aren't right. And I pray that as they speak truth into my life, or seek God to make a decision I wouldn't have picked at first, I'll be humble enough to see God in them. May I always encourage them to seek His voice over mine.

I AM A "C", I AM A "C-H", I AM A "C-H-R-I-S-T-I-A-N"

"I have C-H-R-I-S-T in my H-E-A-R-T and I will L-I-V-E E-T-E-R-N-A-L-L-Y!" This song, which we would sing faster and faster until everyone tripped over the words, gives a teeny window into my young childhood. I can still recall childhood jingles that taught me everything from the importance of patience to the books of the New Testament in order (I apologize if you are singing halfway to Revelation right now).

And let's not forget about "Sword Drills": We held our Bible in the air waiting for someone to call out a Bible verse reference, then we'd race to be the first to find the verse. (Oh, and if you used those little Bible book tabs, you were *so* cheating.)

Some childhood songs and Bible learning could be construed as indoctrination or oversimplification at best. But even though I laugh with my siblings now over some of our religious upbringing, there are so many things I quietly absorbed with the mind of a child that I could not possibly have seen the value of until later.

Though I don't agree with all the ways I learned about Christianity, there are parts of my beginnings that gave me a solid foundation for the genuine faith I have today. Learning Bible verses was one of those foundations.

Once my dad actually made a list of about eighty verses that had come to have special meaning for him over the years. He gave me and my siblings each a copy then offered to pay us a dollar for every verse from the list that we memorized. Just as getting allowance for doing chores ultimately trains kids in responsibility and money management, my parents knew that Biblical truths would far outlast the dollars we earned.

As an adult now, I have this wealth of verses that comes to mind and speaks so clearly into my circumstances. Having solid Biblical knowledge helped me as I grew to better investigate my faith and what it meant to me. The less we know about the basis for what we believe, the less confident we are in our faith. The less we know about God's promises, the less likely we are to claim them and walk in them as adults or to make an independent decision about what we believe at all.

Aside from just memorizing Scripture, I was encouraged to study the Bible on my own from an early age. In some ways it was horrifying: there are some stories in the Old Testament that are horribly violent or downright scandalous! (If you thought Desperate Housewives was bad, you should read about Lot's daughters in Genesis 19.)

Other parts simply seemed perplexing or upsetting. I remember once coming to my Dad asking what on earth God *really* thinks about women- because there seemed to be an awful lot of conflicting verses out there. Instead of giving me an answer, he gave me a bunch of verses to study on my own so I could form my own understanding.

I found that when two Bible verses seem to contradict each other, you have to look at the context of the verse as well as step back and look at how the verses relate to the Bible as a whole. I learned how dangerous it can be to pick one verse out of the atmosphere, without context, because the meaning can become so twisted.

Moreover, I came to find that, even when I don't fully understand the Bible, the truths it teaches are how I want my life to look: free of anxiety, characterized by peace and joy, full of love and grace, focused on others- on justice and compassion.

The Bible may be enigmatic at times, but I can't shake the parts that are not just inspirational but practical. The more I read, the less I'm able to deny the life the words give or to shake my belief that there's more to this whole God thing than just rules and dusty history. More than just "good Christianity". Just as watching my parents follow God forced me to rethink Christianity, learning to study the Bible ensured that I'd *wrestle* with faith for myself.

I learned to test every speaker, book, or philosophy, against the Bible for myself, and not just ideas outside of Christianity. Because even though as parents we may worry about what unhealthy ideas our kids are picking up from the larger culture, how often do we stop to think about the unhealthy ideas they might be getting from the Christian culture? I've found that what I see of God's heart in scripture isn't always accurately portrayed by the larger (or most vocal) Christian community.

I quickly discovered that believing in God doesn't mean I must subscribe to all the ways Christianity is lived or portrayed by others. We're all human so we can't help bringing that into our faith; but I want my faith to always be based on seeking truth, not other people's opinion. So when culture, even (or especially) Christian culture, throws something at me that shakes me or doesn't make sense, I know where to go to find my truth.

EXPERIMENT #1:

Write a summary of your own life story- be as brief or detailed as you want. Consider how your childhood laid the foundation for your current identity and beliefs. Allow yourself to dwell on the emotions that arise and give yourself permission to question things that you may have been afraid to question. There's no right or wrong in this space; you are simply an explorer, searching through your past to find pieces of who you are today. As you write, ask God to begin to show you where your faith might be a bit plastic or built on certain assumptions of the Christianity or faith you grew up with. If you feel comfortable, share your story with a friend or your small group.

2
GRAY CHRISTIAN CULTURE

POP-CHRISTIANITY?

We tell our kids to think for themselves, that it's dangerous to follow the "crowd mentality". It's easy to see the destruction that awaits if our kids follow others into substance abuse, bullying, and materialism. But it becomes much harder to teach kids not to "follow the crowd" if the crowd is made up of Christians. In fact, adults seem to struggle with this as well. In a world that doesn't necessarily follow our values and beliefs, we want to find security in a larger community that thinks as we do.

This is natural, and in some ways quite healthy. But inevitably, even in a Christian community, there are certain ideals or beliefs that become so widely accepted that we stop thinking critically about them. We stop asking whether these ideas or practices are healthy or not- whether they draw people closer to God or push them away.

Especially when we feel like God's honor and values are on the line, we tend to run a bit too hastily into a Christian huddle, make a snap judgement, and run with it "in God's name" without much critical thinking.

For example, in 2012 Dan Cathy, the owner of Chick-Fil-A, stated his company's belief in the Biblical view of marriage as being between a man and woman. Those who support same-sex marriage were, not surprisingly, offended and decided to boycott Chick-Fil-A.

What happened next boggled my mind: Christians picked a day to counter the boycott and came out of the woodworks to "support" Cathy's statement and his company's value system. Or something like that. Or were they supporting God's honor? Actually, I'm not sure anyone knows. Because from my perspective, I could have sworn I watched a bunch of Christians support Christian capitalism and our right to take offense when someone else is offended by us. The nerve.

I'm not here to vilify people for supporting Chick-Fil-A, but I have some questions about our motivation. Did anyone who bought from Chick-Fil-A that day think through what their end goal was? Was it to live out God's heart? Was it to prove something to a world that needs God? If so, what did it prove? Did anyone stop to think what our actions spoke loud and clearly to the LGBT community?

Unfortunately, situations like this solidify the idea that Christians are more known for what they are against than what they are for.

We also have a habit of turning people who think differently than we do into enemies. We can make thoughtless or sweeping statements about other cultures, religions, political views and more. We must learn to live the balance of not conforming to the pattern of the world,[1] while still loving the world as God did.[2] After all, Jesus didn't come to earth with picket signs to boycott sinfulness; he embodied a better way to live and died for sinners before any of us acknowledged Him.[3]

Even when our group actions or widely accepted "Christian-isms" aren't pushing people away from God, sometimes we have to see whether they're really drawing people closer to Him or if we're simply perpetuating a false view of what it means to follow God.

Christian culture often implies that honoring God means exclusively supporting anything that is labeled "Christian", whether TV shows, athletes, businesses or holidays. But people like the Duggars and Robertsons and other "popular" Christians are just as broken as the rest of us and the world sees that. And we may choose to avoid Halloween or minimize Santa at Christmas, but can we do that in a way that doesn't condemn the world or steal the joy from celebrations?

When a legitimate time comes to take a strong stand, can we stop to ask God how to do that in a way that's Biblical and doesn't alienate people? There are many times I look at apparently "popular" Christianity and think that I want no part of that, and I'm not surprised those outside our faith don't want in either. It makes me wonder what God thinks of our version of Christianity.

BIBLE HISTORY & BAD GUYS

A friend who also grew up in the church recently mentioned that for the longest time it didn't occur to her that the history she learned in church overlapped with the history she learned in school. I was excited to hear someone else say that, because I had the exact same thought growing up. I referred to the history I learned in "Sunday School" as "Bible times", while the history I learned in school was just history. I'm not sure if I thought of Bible times as pre-dating regular history, or if I just imagined the Bible on a concurrent but separate timeline. Either way, I was confused.

Around seventh grade I went to a home-school co-op once a week, and one of my teachers assigned us historical fiction reading as part of our curriculum. We read a book called *The Bronze Bow* which follows the life of a Jewish boy in Jesus' time who was torn between the kingdom Jesus preached and those who wanted to physically overthrow the oppressive reign of the Romans. It was enlightening to see Bible history interwoven with "secular" history.

If merging my history timelines was vital to grounding my faith in reality, why did it take me so long? I wonder if part of the issue is the dichotomy of school and church- we see the former as giving us knowledge and facts that pertain to our physical world, and we've come to see the latter as giving us knowledge and insights that pertain to our faith or the spiritual world. We believe that both places offer truth, but our compartmentalization of learning gives us the sense that the truths don't ever overlap.

But if we don't think of Moses and Peter and Jesus as all being in the same long timeline as Cleopatra and Gandhi and President Roosevelt, then our faith is stunted. If God's story doesn't fit into history, where does it fit in at all? We may lament that schools don't teach creationism or Biblical values in class, but for better or worse we can't expect that. The weight of helping our kids understand how the Bible fits in with history falls on us.

Another negative concept I absorbed in Sunday school was that there are always clearly designated bad guys and good guys. The Old Testament certainly calls nations or people "enemies" of God, but the truth is that most of the Bible is about people who sometimes chose to obey God, and sometimes didn't. When we call some people "bad" and others "good" we're promoting "good Christianity"- undermining our universal need for

God's grace.

And when we hear a simplified Bible story, don't we naturally tend to associate with the "good" guy- with the hero of the story? Don't we tend to easily point out the bad things that other characters are doing without considering that we might exhibit some of those same negative traits?

Take the Pharisees, for example: we've pretty much vilified these religious leaders of Jesus' time. And why not? They were self-righteous, proud, and had a huge hand in killing Jesus. In fact, I remember reading one Bible passage where Jesus heals a man right in front of the Pharisees.[4] Everyone is becoming a Jesus groupie and it makes the pharisees so angry that they decide then and there that he must die.

So to recap: Jesus heals a guy- Pharisees want to kill him for it.

Ultimately their anger and jealousy towards Jesus twisted His good healing into a negative thing, into fuel for their hatred. Then came a little uninvited conviction: I was alarmed to find that I'd acted the same way towards people in my life, unable to acknowledge any of their good because of my frustration. I've actually wished negative things for people in my anger. *Yikes.* Sometimes I have the most to learn from the "bad guys".

Thankfully, church clearly taught me that "good guys" of the Bible still made mistakes- I knew growing up that even the good aren't perfect and need God. But did my rigid view of the Bible's "bad guys" keep me from fully seeing myself as a "bad guy" too- just as broken and in need of help as the next guy?

I wonder if identifying as a "good guy" keeps me from seeing in myself the errors and pitfalls that are at the root of those who made the Bible's "bad guy" list. Do I sometimes do my own kids a disservice by trying to oversimplify ideas in the Bible? Allowing ourselves to fully see our own desperate need for grace means recognizing our inner bad-guy tendencies, even if it stings our pride.

QUESTIONING THE BUBBLE

My sophomore year of high school I joined a small Christian based theater class (a slice of bright in my world), and an equally Christian branch of "Toast Masters", a public speaking class. Of all the life-skills we were learning, we seemed to be missing the one about what it means to breathe life into the real world instead of creating a parallel but separate culture in Christianity.

I vividly remember a girl in class being asked to share something she was thankful for. The summary of her answer was that she was so grateful to her parents for sheltering her from the world and all the negative things therein. In that moment, it was as though I saw our group from the outside. All I could think was that this was all wrong- we weren't meant to be completely sheltered from the world, and maybe it wasn't all as bad as we all thought.

I began to feel as though I didn't belong in any of my worlds entirely- I didn't feel entirely comfortable with people outside my faith, but I increasingly felt at odds with the just-rightness of the isolated Christian culture that I seemed to be a part of.

As odd as it sounds, the ongoing questioning of Christian culture was vital to maintaining my faith. I didn't feel at ease in some Christian circles with good reason. There was part of the world, part of the truth of God that I wasn't seeing; there were a lot of closed-minded attitudes that blocked out the positive culture with the negative. God allowed me to see that not all of the Christianity I was experiencing was right or best.

With everything in my being I want to preserve my children's innocence, simplicity and joy as long as I can. We're actually in the middle of a trial year of homeschooling my own kids, partly because I want them to be confident in God before they're bombarded with the values and priorities of the world. At the same time, I want to expose them to a wide variety of ideas and people interactions because I don't want Christian culture to be all they're aware of.

It wasn't until I returned to public school that I really got to *interact* on a regular basis with people who believed differently from me. All the books I could read on other beliefs did not make me an expert on someone else's thoughts; true understanding comes not from conjecture or research but from engaging with real people.

Conversely, others can think they know our Christianity schtick inside and out, but they'll never know our real story until we are real and present enough to share it. If I'm actively raising my kids in a Christian environment, I need to learn to trust that foundation enough to let my kids experience people from a wide variety of backgrounds and philosophies. That may mean homeschool isn't the best option for my kids forever. I hope to be just as vigilant about raising my children to find faith as I am about letting them interact with a world outside their own- outside the Christian bubble.

MARKETING JESUS

After tenth grade, my dad applied for a pastoring job in a little town in Connecticut, and once again we packed up our lives and moved. I somewhat nervously returned to public school for my junior year of high school. One day in class, I remember searching my backpack for something to write with and feeling somewhat horrified by the one pencil I was able to scrounge up. How did I let *THAT* pencil come to school with me? It was blue with festive little snowmen in red hats- a pencil that would have been cute to me if the little balls of snow stood solo. But along with the snowmen, all over the pencil was plastered the phrase, *"Jesus Loves You Snow Much."* Oh snow much! A friend of mine saw it, and playfully laughed, but the deep and true meaning of that phrase-turned-pun was hardly felt.

I was embarrassed by that pencil, to be honest. I won't say that I was embarrassed of *Jesus*, but of all the plastic Christian veneer the pencil represented- of the cheapened way that Jesus had been "marketed" in my generation.

Marketed.

I really don't think that's too strong a word for some of the ways that we as Christians have tried to share or promote our faith. If nothing else, some of our attempts to show Jesus to the world come off like little more than a glorified political campaign. We have religious bumper stickers and Jesus fishies, smiley face "Jesus loves you" stickers, WWJD bracelets - I've even seen massive billboards on highways with "messages" from God and lawn signs designed to draw people into churches. I'm not saying that all these things are wrong, but for myself, having seen them my whole life, they've become somewhat more disturbing to me than comforting.

What is their purpose? Are we trying to promote our God or our church? Do we put a Jesus fishy on our car to shout to the world that we're a Christian? Or is it so we can spot our fellow Christians while we are out and about and feel a sense of unity? Are they just meant to be cute reminders of God for us and our children?

If we're honest, is it sometimes easier to display outward signs of our faith than to focus on the inside? Do we let our Christian paraphernalia do our talking so we don't have to? And if all our Jesus stuff is talking, what is it saying to a world that desperately needs hope?

Why was I really embarrassed by that pencil? Although I believed in Jesus, sometimes *even I* felt like the message was empty. "Jesus loves you", one of the most profound truths of the Bible, had been so simply and repetitively packaged as to become trite. Despite, or perhaps precisely because of, the constant repetition of that phrase, I've grasped God's love for me at an intellectual level, but I still struggle to accept that love in reality. It has taken me into my adulthood to even begin to embrace the reality of that love, and I still have moments of doubt.

The funny thing is, I now have three kids of my own and almost daily I remind them that God loves them. I pray over them night after night that they will know Jesus and His vast love for them. Because I get it - as parents we want that idea to be redundant enough to penetrate their worldview. The question is, how do we let that them *experience* that concept?

I'm not really sure I have the answer. But it begins with realizing that we can't talk a concept that mysterious and wonderful into their hearts. I certainly believe we should speak that truth into their lives often. But each child, each person we encounter, must realize the depth of that love for themselves through their own interaction with God and His people. What does it look like to be relational signposts of God and His kingdom? An experience with God is what people need- and that is something we can't manufacture, mass produce, or market.

ADULTS ON STRIKE

Although I desire diversity and independent thinking for my children, I get that sometimes we have to draw strong lines for our kids. We can't put them in front of a buffet at age four, for instance, and tell them to "use their judgement" when choosing dinner. We shouldn't be surprised if they skip straight to the dessert table or get a whole plate of cheese fries. Parent-enforced rules are obviously a healthy tool for our kids until they're ready for more independence. But independence must always come, and that same kid at age ten should be trying the buffet for himself, even if he has to learn the hard way that three plates of greasy food will catch up with him later.

Yet I'm often surprised by the number of adult Christians that don't know how to think independently or walk in spiritual tension. I think that's a part of our sometimes fearful Christian culture. It's as though many still live under the mindset that we must avoid all ideas that we don't fully agree with because just a little exposure might ruin us or confuse us.

There are whole Christian groups that rally together in opposition of a particular author, for instance, because of his apparently sacrilegious take on spirituality. Or heaven forbid, they say, we read ideas and beliefs written by those outside the Christian faith. If we write off these books and authors, we often also criticize anyone who reads them at all. Some act as though digesting the wrong books or ideas makes a person less godly, proof that one has gone off the spiritual deep end.

But I'd like to suggest quite the opposite- *that someone who exposes themselves to viewpoints that they don't necessarily agree with might actually be in a healthier place in their faith than someone who avoids any tension.*

In history class my senior year of high school, my teacher said, "If you could absolutely disprove Christianity, you wouldn't do it." He explained that people orient their whole lives around their religion and it gives them a sense of comfort for what they can't explain in life and death. So even if we could categorically debunk religion, would we really do it only to leave people hopeless? Only to take away their sense of identity and security?

Maybe some want religion as a sort of fairy tale to make them feel OK now, but I have to disagree. Paul says quite emphatically, "If only for this life we have hope in Christ, we are of all people most to be pitied."[5] I'm not ultimately looking to religion that gives me warm fuzzies now and has no power over my future; I'm looking for the truth. Understanding other beliefs doesn't change truth and experiencing other ideas doesn't alter truth. If truth is what I have then nothing will shake that, and if in any way I'm lacking truth, I'd rather find it than hold onto something plastic.

At best my research gives me greater relatability to others and confirms my faith, at worst it leaves me questioning and seeking to learn more. At the end of the day, I just want to be closer to the truth.

That thirst for truth also gives me freedom to read a variety of opposing viewpoints from within Christianity itself. I'm not entirely sure what makes us so inflexible in our pursuit of learning about God. Sometimes in our effort to stand firm in our faith, we pretend there are no areas of ambiguity in the Bible- we act as though there are no gray spaces within our faith.

We somehow buy into the idea that to have questions or doubts means something is wrong with us. Perhaps we fear that God won't honor our faith if we can't stuff those questions somewhere deep inside and leave them to rot. Or what if we never take the first step to belief because we feel that to believe means we have to ignore the parts of faith we don't understand?

But suppose we look at it a different way- God is big enough for our questions and fears, and only when we trust Him with our honest searching do we find ourselves moving closer to His heart. So is it OK to wonder about hell, to ask if homosexuality is really wrong, to be overwhelmed by the severity of God's punishment at times? Is it normal to wonder why God doesn't stop suffering or to wrestle with Jesus and the mystery of his human deity?

I believe it's more than OK. I believe we give God our honest selves, and He meets us in the questions.

Part of becoming mature in our faith is learning to test everything that we read and hear for ourselves according to the Bible and the Spirit. I've come to find that there's no one speaker or author that I agree with 100%, and even in my own thinking there are flaws. But far from banning myself from hearing from partly-wrong people, I find I thrive on a diversity of ideas.

Each of us has a unique experience with God or life to share; each of us has different questions and insights that others need to hear. Even when I read something that I staunchly disagree with, it makes me go back to the Bible and ask, "Why?". Do I disagree with this idea because I was taught it was wrong, or do I really have grounds to discredit it? Are the Bible verses that talk about this subject straightforward, or is it, in fact, one of those gray areas? Maybe I'm mistaken or at least have room to grow.

Finally, if we're unable to hear other ideas and beliefs, why would we ask that of people with whom we wish to share our faith? I mean, if we're hoping that others will seriously contemplate our thoughts, shouldn't we give more than a half-hearted nod at what they're sharing about their life? Sharing our faith isn't supposed to be a one-way exchange in which we give someone all the "right" answers to life.

Even Jesus, who IS embodied truth, would stop and have conversations- dialogue- with people. When He met the woman at the well in Samaria, He didn't come right out and tell her that He was the Savior of the world. She shared her beliefs with Him, her partly-right thoughts on salvation and faith, and He let her ask questions and think about the truth for herself.[6]

If we never hear any perspectives other than those that mirror our own, at best we'll be severely stunted in our understanding of Christ and this thing we call love.

LOST IN TRANSLATION

When I was 18, I remember hanging out with a couple of friends from my high school. We'd known each other long enough that they knew I believed in God, but that night they started talking with me a little more about my faith. One friend asked me:

"So, are you a *born again* Christian?"

Long pause.

I wasn't sure what they meant. Suddenly the phrase had an ominous sound to it. I mean, if anyone from church asked me if I was "born again" I'd say, "Yes!", because church people say that like it's a good thing. When church people say this, they're probably referring to John 3:3 where Jesus says that to be in the Kingdom of God you must be "born again." But even the people Jesus was talking to were confused, and how the phrase became so popular I can't fathom.

"Um, I guess? Well, what do you mean by 'born again'?" I replied, awkwardly.

I forget the exact conversation that followed, but the punchline was that they both thought of "born again" Christians as judgmental fanatics- probably the kind of over-zealous, fire-happy people that burn down anything that opposes their beliefs.

'Ah, soooo, no. I'll make my answer no. I'm just a regular Christian. Just born the one time.'

Honestly, I'm not surprised the term "born again" is confusing to people, but I was surprised at what a harsh picture friends outside my church had associated with it. I knew that some of our church language wasn't obvious to the world, but I didn't realize people outside the church might have made up their own definition to the words in our dictionary.

The whole conversation was a fresh reminder that people need a translator to decode much of our Christian lingo. When you grow up in a Christian environment you get so used to common Christian language and traditions that you forget they aren't universal.

My husband helped me realize this; he grew up believing in God but didn't go to church often. I remember talking to him once about how I didn't listen to much "secular" music growing up, and he chuckled and said, "We just call that music."

What a strange thought. I guess not everyone got the memo that once the Christians started their own music category, everything else was automatically secular. (Oh, and don't even get me started on the flack Christian artists get when they "go secular".)

We can keep our isms and sayings all we want, but when we go out and speak our language to the world, we'd better make sure they're hearing what we're actually saying. And frankly, I feel the need to reexamine some of the more routine phrases of my faith for myself so I know exactly what they are saying to *me*. I can get so used to talking about being "saved" by the "blood of the Lamb" or about how I'm "blessed" to live in "God's economy" that I lose the meaning entirely.

The phrases themselves can become worn out and annoyingly predictable so I have to ask God to help my heart to really hear again. Allowing God and His Word to maintain an active and fresh place in my life when faith feels routine is one of the hardest things about growing up in Christian culture.

EXPERIMENT #2:

Sometimes we struggle to be constructively critical of our faith backgrounds and the Christian culture around us. To question might feel like we're letting our parents, churches, or even God down. But Jesus Himself challenged the status quo of the faith culture of His time, and sometimes our own faith culture drifts away from God's heart as well. Even when it comes to following Christian leaders, Paul doesn't ask us to blindly copy- he says to first "consider the outcome of their way of life" (Hebrews 13:7). Translation: reflect before following.

Jesus says that we, His sheep, will know His voice and follow- but I think that means sometimes silencing the sounds of the other sheep in our heads. Make space this week to sit and talk with God alone, away from distractions. Ask Him to help you hear His voice, to give you discernment, and be able to distinguish His will outside of what any culture says. Allow yourself to ask whether you've been sometimes following people instead of God.

3
GRAY CHURCH

COOL CHURCH, COOL GOD?

For many years I had an inborn pride in going to a church that my dad started from the ground up in Massachusetts. Our weekly gatherings began very simply in my house with my parents leading most "ministries", then grew into a school auditorium with a worship team and a significant children's group.

Because I was never "new" to church, I never thought much about what our church would seem like to someone who walked in for the first time. I didn't stop to consider much whether my church presented itself in a culturally relevant or attractive way. And while we certainly sought to be relatable to the larger world, it wasn't until my family's big move to Alabama that I was truly introduced to the concept of a "seeker friendly" church.

I walked into the church from the outside, and saw with new eyes. My Alabama church had a full band complete with lead vocalists, guitarists, and drummer. They would sometimes set up the auditorium seating with chairs at round tables, cafe style, instead of in rows. We employed the latest technology, video clips, and frequent live skit illustrations. A message series might revolve around a current popular movie or TV show like *The Lord of the Rings* or *Who Wants to be a Millionaire*. I suddenly found myself at Church 2.0- "cool church".

Though the church was very much seeking to honor God through its cultural relevance, somewhere along the way I got it in my head that "cool church" was necessary to get people to know God. "Cool church" somehow made our God seem cooler, as though God were only as relevant as our church service. Perhaps God needed our PR to make Him attractive, to give Him credibility with mainstream culture.

So my pride in my church now stemmed from the idea that I was part of something that was modern and dynamic, where even the pastors might wear jeans. (I know. Be still my soul.) I became convinced that other churches were missing the mark or even putting Christians in a bad light by wearing dresses and suits, singing hymns and preaching long-winded sermons.

Though in some ways I needed to see the church body as vibrant and creative, colorful and accessible to the outside world, WHAT the church looked like became bigger than WHO created the church.

Try though we might, we cannot *make* God more or less relevant. He is the "I AM"[1]- He's constant and unchanging, yesterday, today and tomorrow.[2] He. Is. Relevant. Period. Why? Because He offers what the world in all its brokenness never can. He offers eternal life, yes, but He also offers peace, joy, love, and hope for this life.

If the world could find those deepest longings fulfilled in the surrounding culture- in the world- then it wouldn't need the church- it wouldn't need God.

We can use music and entertainment, technology and pop culture references as tools to connect people to God, but none of it matters unless we leave room for God's presence. None of it matters if being relevant eclipses the Object of our worship-- if we try to humanly manufacture what only God can create.

Further, if God's presence alone can sustain the church, I think we need to clarify what it means to be a "seeker friendly" church. If the goal is to create an environment where a new person can walk in at any point and feel welcomed and comfortable, then fantastic. Can we use seating and lighting, technology and music to facilitate that? Yes. I'm more convinced than ever that our church should seek to engage the larger culture, which means being willing to adapt over time and actively pursue a welcoming environment that connects with those in our unique communities.

I'm equally convinced that cultural relevancy isn't enough, and that "seeker friendly" can only take us so far. Even if someone comes to church because it's inviting and upbeat, modern or disarmingly trendy, eventually they're going to be uncomfortable. Because the church is a community of people, and people are messy. People aren't always kind, loving, and selfless.

When community gets real, when we get past the surface, there are disagreements and hurts, mistakes and misunderstandings. Trendy church isn't going to entice me to stay when inevitable problems arise. But if we're a church that seeks God above pleasing people, there should also be a sense of love and care for each other that is not quite so common in the world today. Relevancy may attract me, but an encounter with God and a community of authenticity- genuine love- is what keeps me engaged.

Even if our church community were perfect, people SHOULD still be uncomfortable sooner or later. Because, frankly, the message of Christ isn't a comfortable one. If you think about it, Jesus offended more people than followed Him. If truth is being taught- eventually all of us will encounter a level of discomfort that challenges our human nature- that asks us to give up ourselves.

Jesus said that whoever wants to follow Him should "deny themselves and take up their cross daily".[3] God offers us all of Himself, but He requires all of me- all of you- in return. The longer we follow Him, the more we will see the layers of our comfort, security, and selfishness peeled away. In short, following God is countercultural which by definition isn't trendy. We don't need to avoid expressions of modern culture in our church, but that should never become a veneer that mutes uninhibited surrender to God.

So how do we do "seeker friendly" *and* life-changing? Where's the intersection of welcoming and challenging? Is there room for God in our "cool churches"? Do we really believe that God will always be relevant to people no matter what our church looks like?

GET ME TO CHURCH

I was a little rule-following nine year old, headed to my first AWANA (Approved Workmen Are Never Ashamed) meeting with a friend from church. It's kind of like the Christian version of Girl or Boy Scouts. As we walked in the church double doors, I peered in at the bright colorful tape on the floor in the next room marking where we would sit and play games as a group. I was a "Spark" as I would later find out, who would have to earn badges and gems for my pin by memorizing Bible verses and meeting other goals.

My friend signed in as a regular, and I registered as a guest of hers. I remember she got a special prize for bringing a friend (although as a pastor's kid, I'm fairly certain I was not the target friend the prize was meant to fetch).

It strikes a chord in me today that many Christian groups use incentives to get Christian kids to invite and reach out to their presumably unsaved friends. If a child comes to know Christ because a friend of hers really wants to earn a prize- what's the harm?

My fear, from living through it, is that children growing up in the church are constantly soaking in messages about how to live out faith based on what adults model or teach. Are we instilling in kids the idea that the motivation for "evangelism" or reaching out to a friend who may not know God, is something for ourselves?

It's almost like selling Girl Scout cookies- as kids we don't necessarily see the value of raising money for our group, but we're all about earning individual prizes for what we sell. If prizes help raise more money for your troupe, then the end seems to justify the means. But even if prizes bring in more kids to church, is there a negative attached? A cost for our children's mindset in the long run?

The early church certainly held incentive for people to join, but it was a built in benefit: a radical community that loved each other like family and gave everything for each other.[4] That was amazingly attractive, and still is for people today. I laugh trying to picture the disciples in a panic, strategizing how to get more people in the church doors. *"Paul! We're all out of mini clay Jesus jars for the children, how will we get them to bring more friends?"*

But joking aside, I believe the more subtly dangerous message we send to adults and children alike is that getting a child to a Christian event is the most effective way to reach them. Is that true? What about people who will never enter a church once in their life? What about people who have entered many churches and have been too hurt to return?

Christians may reinforce the idea that WE are the church- that the people, and not a building, are together the hands and feet of Christ. We claim that where two or three are gathered in His name, Jesus is there.[5] Our presence in the community is bringing and being a light to the world because Jesus miraculously lives in us.

But at the same time, there's often a strong emphasis on inviting non-Christians to church, getting involved in church ministries, and bringing friends to church events. The subtle and unintended message is that a person who doesn't know God would best find Him within the church *building* or within the context of a church event.

One of the side effects of this thinking is that we copy the larger culture in our attempts to engage people outside our walls. We host Christian movie nights, Christian concert outings, church softball games: you fill in the blank. The issue again isn't that these things are inherently wrong, but do they keep us from leaving our walls and being the church in organizations and functions that already exist in the public? What if we joined or started groups that weren't necessarily "sponsored" or put on by the church? Think books clubs, town sports leagues, theater groups, library story time for kids.

If we find that all of our time is devoted to church run events and ministries, we need to evaluate our hearts. Are we motivated to change lives for eternity, but unsure of how to do that outside of the church? If I'm honest, often I'm nervous or concerned about how to reach out to others without the security of a church ministry. How long have I subtly believed that a Sunday morning service, complete with pastors and free coffee, is really the best way to impact someone? As believers we have to become comfortable with the idea of being the church outside the building, and modeling that for our kids.

THESE FOUR WALLS

From my earliest days I was involved in the church. It never even occurred to me to ask to stay home on a Sunday. Seriously. I relished feeling like I was on the inside of this living organism called church. As a kid my dad would sometimes ask me or my siblings if he could use a story from our lives as a sermon illustration, and I ate that stuff up. In my own little world I felt like the president's daughter- proud to be a pastor's kid.

It didn't hurt that I was best friends with the daughter of our church's music director for many years as well. So I never had to seek out being involved in church volunteering- I was just there. If they needed a couple kids to sing, I was asked- I even remember singing a "special" with the adults once just because practice happened to be at my house.

Through the years I've helped with drama, vacation Bible school (VBS), nursery, children's ministry, bulletin folding, and worship team to name a few. I'm not trying to wow you with my church serving resume- I'm making the point that from my youngest days I lived and breathed church.

In fact, it didn't occur to me until the last few years just how attached I was to being an automatic fixture in the church. My dad stopped pastoring my current church in late 2011, and my parents have again moved across the country to Alabama. (They're kind of getting predictable now.) I've had a more painful experience transitioning than I would've expected, and part of that is the loss of being on the inside of everything church as I once was.

I'm probably more involved in the church now than ever, but for awhile I felt like part of my church identity was missing. I'm the only one of my family still attending, which is genuinely hard when you've grown up with church being a family thing. But I also wrestled through this feeling of being less in the loop with what was happening in the church. I was less likely to be asked to do something because I was in the right place at the right time, less likely to interact with church leaders by virtue of having a leader for a father.

The ramifications of this are still unfolding in my life, but I've realized that for too long I've placed far too much stock in my church identity. I've spent too much time believing that the best or only use of my gifts or talents is within the church service setting, or that my value and identity depend on my performance within church ministry.

More recently I've found myself questioning what my role within the church is even supposed to be. Am I supposed to do something that the church desperately needs volunteers for even if it doesn't seem like the best fit for me? Perhaps this is what serving others sacrificially means.

Or should I try to find something I'm passionate about and run with it? Ideally, yes, but what happens when I'm not currently needed in the role that I wanted or the church isn't able to support my ministry dream right now? This may sound petty, but we in the church are still susceptible to jealousy, selfishness, and insecurity. How do we learn to accept our roles in humility and love?

Further, how do we allow ourselves to shift roles in different seasons of our lives? Kids, illness, relationships, job situations, depression and more affect what we're able to do. How do we give ourselves the space to reflect on what's healthy for us, and the grace to say no to things without guilt? What does it really mean to serve the body of Christ in love and to be served?

I very much believe that the local church- the body of believers- is a beautiful, mysterious thing and that we're meant to pour out our lives into each other. We need to meet regularly for worship, to experience God, to connect with people and hear from the Word. Church ministry isn't obsolete or unnecessary. We should be loving, serving and encouraging each other in community, and the simple truth is that we might miss community without intentional meetings, volunteering, programs and structure within the church.

But for those of us who've grown up in the church, it's wise if not imperative to take a step back from church ministry at some point every so often, just long enough to ask ourselves why we do it. Does it fuel our sense of identity in an unhealthy way? Is it an excuse for not trying to be involved outside the church? Do I find myself serving to make someone else happy? Is my value too closely tied to my ministry role or whether I feel needed?

Sometimes in asking myself these questions I've found that God needs to do a work in me. He's had to peel off layers of my own self-absorption and pride. I'm learning to acknowledge the beauty of someone else's gift and talent and the way God is using them for His glory. God has shown me that while I'm made to serve in His community, the church can actually run without me and that's a *good* thing. Only when we acknowledge that do we give God the space to reign. Only when He is in control are we able to serve without people-pleasing, insecurity, and selfishness.

Other times, those same questions have lead me to hard conversations with family, friends and church leaders. Sometimes it feels easier to stay in a ministry that isn't working for you than to tell a leader you need to step down. Sometimes you want to be involved, but aren't sure if you agree with how things are being run. Part of being in a healthy community is learning to share our concerns in a healthy way, and learning to respect others when they believe God is leading in a different direction.

Giving ourselves healthy permission to take a break from ministry from time to time allows us that space for reflection that leads to clearer action. We won't be effective in what we do unless we pause (cease ministry) long enough to ask God for His direction and to ensure we're doing what we do for Him and through Him.

DIVISION IN THE CHURCH

I once read a bumper sticker that said, "If it ain't King James, it ain't the Bible". Even as a young teen, I thought to myself, *"Terrific, you not only managed to make Christianity seem legalistic and unappealing to non-Christians, you simultaneously found a way to create division between yourself and thousands of your brothers and sisters whose Bible translation begins in anything other than KJ. Bully for you. Fantastic...really well played."*

The truth is, we in the Christian world have a knack for finding a few things in the Bible that we don't agree on, and building whole denominations or churches based on those differences. Call it an oversimplification, but it's much easier to surround ourselves with people who think just like we do than to live in the tension of a community of believers who differ in the myriad gray issues of our faith.

We differ in how we take communion, how we baptize, how we relate to the Holy Spirit, how we dress, what music is appropriate for worship, whether we say "Amen" or repeat prayers, whether women can be church leaders, and so much more. The list is simply meant to illustrate how very easy it is to find differences among believers, and how easily these lead us to split into groups with others who believe similarly.

One of the ways this has manifested itself for me is a strong pride in my personal church. Such pride, in the right context, is a natural and healthy expression of belonging to a church community in which you see the power of God and where you feel loved, challenged, and accepted. But for me that pride blurred itself into the realm of believing that my church was THE right model with THE right beliefs.

In other words, I unconsciously came to believe that of all the people in the world, of all the churches in the world, our church kind of had a corner on this God thing- as though we had gotten secret blueprints directly from God Himself.

A lot of this was purely my wrong thinking, but it wasn't helped by the fact that I didn't really have a clear context for other churches and denominations. Especially in my very young years, I don't remember that we partnered with other churches often to accomplish larger missions. Since my dad preached most Sundays, we didn't usually have a chance to visit other churches, and if we did they tended to be fairly similar to ours.

I remember one of the first times I visited a more charismatic church with my parents as a middle schooler. I stared, awkwardly, as one woman jumped backwards over and over, as though in a joyful trance, oblivious even to chairs she was bumping into. Having never witnessed that kind of Spirit movement before, I was rather uncomfortable, and it certainly didn't occur to me that OUR church might be missing some of what this church had.

As a teen I finally went to group events or missions trips where at least a variety of church denominations were present. Working together towards a common goal with people from different backgrounds was perhaps the easiest way to lose sight of our differences. The theology and the nuances of denominations quickly get lost in the larger purpose.

Differences actually have the power to sharpen and challenge us when we embrace them in the context of love. Differences force us to return to our most basic faith, to remember again that we're all small and broken and unable to fully grasp who God is and what it means to follow Him. In the end we find that our differences need not keep us from worshipping and serving God together.

In my college years and beyond I've been convicted that church division is not, as I'd once thought, just a pity, but a tragedy of the church. Over and over the Bible talks about unity in the Spirit- unity of mind- love. There shouldn't be fits of jealousy or rage, slander, or finger pointing and selfish ambition:[6] all things that lead to division. Rather we are to love.

Jesus Himself prays for all believers to have the same kind of unity and oneness that He has with God the Father. The result, He says, is that "the world will know that you sent me and have loved them even as you have loved me".[7] What have our divisions done for us? Can we even comprehend the cost of our disunity?

Ultimately, I believe the church isn't just here as a support group for our clan of people. We're supposed to care for one another across racial, ethnic, and economic lines. But when we become too fragmented and focused on our theology or our own needs, we aren't likely aware of the needs of the broader local church, much less the church across the ocean. If the kingdom of heaven is going to be full of people from all nations,[8] many of which are drastically different than us, I wonder what we're missing out on here by separating ourselves.

Though I'm more keenly aware of division now than ever, I admittedly haven't moved much towards change. Where do you start, right? But I can't make excuses for myself because I'm daunted by hard steps. As a simple action, my husband and I are bringing our kids to other churches periodically so they begin to see a fuller picture of the body of Christ. I'm also *learning* to listen to those who disagree with me without being defensive and dismissive. Many of our mountains of disunity are only as tall as our inability to dialogue.

I pray that God collectively gives us wisdom and a strong push towards life-changing unity with other believers. I know unity will always be an ongoing process for me and the church as a whole, but how unimaginably worth it.

LEAVING THE CHURCH…SORT OF

One of the side effects of being a pastor's kid didn't occur to me until I went away to college for the first time: I'd never had to pick a church before. It was a strange experience. I went to one well attended church with massive balconies and a weekly giving total that floored me, and another where someone in my row randomly blew a horn during the service and there was a human prayer tunnel at the end. That was new.

Though I visited several churches while I was away, I always felt like my *real* church family was at home in CT where my dad was preaching every week. But when my parents left that church to move back to Alabama for the second time, I was a married 25 year old with two kids of my own. For once I couldn't just pick up my life and follow theirs.

In some unconscious way, I began to feel that now if I stayed at church it was an adult choice, not a natural byproduct of being where my parents were. But having to *choose* church forced me to really think through what I believed church should look like. It was hard to be critical of church direction and structure when my dad was teaching because I had such an amazing relationship with him and respect forged through a couple decades.

It wasn't that I never questioned things- but I could always talk concerns out, and I had that built in pride in church because it represented my family. Oddly enough, when my parents moved, I suddenly found myself questioning even church issues that had been going on long before my dad left- things that I was simply never objective enough to put under scrutiny.

One of the hardest things I've ever done is stepping down completely from all ministry as my husband and I backed away from the church to wrestle though our questions and issues. In that season I let go of both the ministry that drained me and the ministry I absolutely loved, and so for a time I let go of whatever identity I derived from either.

I'm not proud of all my actions during that time, because I let emotions cause me to react and feed into division. Still, I think I needed the experience of letting go of church long enough to feel like I was choosing for myself. I needed to give myself permission to question.

Of course, in questioning a few things, I found myself questioning everything: *What is the modern church supposed to look like? Have we drifted too far from how the early Church in Acts looked, or can we remotely expect 21st century church to look that way? Are we too program focused? Should we try to be especially open and inviting to possible newcomers or trust that a raw encounter with God is what a newcomer is really seeking? What would that raw encounter even look like?*

Should church be more family centered, and how should we involve and engage our kids at church as they grow older? How much money should we give towards missions, and what price, if any, is too high for programs or services put on by the church? How much voice should church members have in the leadership decisions? Should females be allowed more active leadership roles in the church? What does the church look like to those outside the church and why?

These questions and more nagged at us as we spent at least two months contemplating church issues.

We wrestled with different ideas and churches and ultimately decided to stay at our original church, though we never answered all of our questions. In fact, one of the things that helped us make a renewed commitment was the simple realization that no one church would be able to meet all our expectations or satisfy all our questions. If we started over somewhere else, how long before we became disgruntled or disillusioned by church members again? And what of our relational and kingdom investments would we be giving up by starting over?

Another unforeseen reason to stay was being placed with our now adopted son. We'd been waiting so long for this baby, and it occurred to me that the body of people at our church felt the most like long-time family- family that I wanted to share this new life with. At a relational level, I felt connected to this church in a very beautiful way as our closest and deepest relationships had been forged here. I trusted the hearts of those friends and the love they had for God and each other. Maybe the relationships were all I needed to feel OK about church again.

So after our decision to stay I breathed a sigh of relief and naively believed that maybe church doubt and questions would never flare up for me again. Unfortunately that simply wasn't the case, and for many weeks it was still hard to walk through those church doors. At times I still feel disappointed, lost, or critical, even though I sense that God is there and actively working.

After probably two years of struggling, I'm finally more at peace about church again. What did all my wrestling teach me? One thing I've learned is that church isn't always a place free of pain, free of tension, whether it's my own or someone else's. But that doesn't make it less beautiful or less worthy of support. Often committing to church unity means making sacrifices or sticking around with people that I may not always agree with to honor God. And that means someone else is making a sacrifice for me too.

I'm learning that I have to let my identity be in God alone, that I have to be confident in my position as His daughter, whether I'm the pastor's daughter or not. I'm more convinced than ever that it's OK to question church- in fact, questioning and being willing to change as God moves is exactly how my church got to where it is today. Without questions and discernment, we become stagnant; we play it safe. We stop asking God where He's going.

Another slow realization for me is that church was never meant to fulfill me or you entirely. It's a beautiful expression of unity and community comprised of wonderful but broken people. It's the bride of Christ, yes, but not made perfect yet. In all my searching for "perfect church" I found that it really just doesn't exist.

I need to grow more comfortable expressing my love for my brothers and sisters and the world beyond outside of those four walls. And I should go to church expecting to experience God, but I should expect God just the same the rest of the week, for He dwells within me. If I feel stubborn, critical, or confused sometimes, God still wants to meet with me. And if I ache for something more, if I feel hollow and not quite sure of this thing called church from time to time, that's OK... because what I'm really longing for is heaven.

EXPERIMENT #3:

If you're a regular church attender, and especially if you're very active in your church, plan a time to take a week off. If you feel comfortable, try taking a week off from church altogether. Instead, carve out some time to meet with God on your own or with your family. Worship God in a stripped setting- perhaps out in nature, or a personal favorite place. Understand, this isn't meant to drive you away from your church. Rather, stepping back gives you a chance to breathe in God without feeling the weight of a "role" to perform, and stepping back from routine helps you gain fresh perspective. During this time, honestly give God your ministries, your experience and expectations within the church, your relationships with members and leaders. Ask God to show you where your heart is in line with His and where He wants to shift your heart, roles, or expectations. Write down your thoughts from this reflection.

4
GRAY SIN

THE "BIG SINS"

As a kid I was taught that we did *not* evolve from monkeys- that we were created with a purpose by a master Designer. In school I would listen to my teacher talk about the earth being billions of years old and I would smugly think to myself that I had one up on all the schmucks that believed this load of crap. (Except I wasn't allowed to use that word until much later in my life.)

In first grade Mrs. G would go on about how the ice caps or glaciers melted to form the seas, and we'd eventually move onto dinosaurs and their Jurassic or Cretaceous periods. Clearly I didn't pay enough attention at the time. I think I figured out a way to filter out or compartmentalize all the science that I didn't personally believe in while still maintaining my A average. The stuff that raised questions, like, "How does evidence of actual dinosaur bones fit in with Adam and Eve or Noah's ark?", I just pushed to the back of my mind. There's a reason, it all makes sense somehow.

La, la, la.

When I returned to public school my junior year in high school, I believed that every good Christian kid should be ready to debate intelligent design (the theory that God or a higher being created the earth) with their classmates. To me it was easier to debate evolution than to share my faith story with my friends- and I felt like I was playing with all these indisputable facts, because that's how intelligent design had always been taught to me.

But the truth is, the story of how we all arrived on this planet cannot be satisfactorily proven, one way or another. Further, I don't think that my arguing ever made a blessed bit of difference. I'd leave a debate more sure than ever that I was right and everyone who disagreed was blind. But I bet they thought the same thing.

Why did I do it? To be honest, at some level it felt like a moral obligation- would I be a religious pansy if I sat and listened to something I didn't believe in and didn't put my two opposing cents in? But I think there was more to it than that- "evolution" became synonymous in my mind with everything that was secular, opposing my faith, against Christ.

If I fought for creationism, I was proving my loyalty to Christ in a detached, impersonal way- if I won the argument (which never really happened) I would have surely won someone over to my faith. Somehow disproving evolution became the way to convince someone of Christ- but it also became almost more important to me than the person with whom I was arguing. More important than Jesus?

Aside from evolution, I grew up believing that to oppose certain big "no-nos" of Christianity made me somehow a champion of God's cause. Abortion and homosexuality were two of the big ones. If someone asked me about abortion I would answer matter-of-factly that it was 100% wrong and absolutely atrocious. A friend brought up abortion once, and she was surprised by how quickly my usually mild manner turned to strong reaction.

Similarly, if someone asked what I thought about homosexuality, I thought I had an easy answer. I once believed what I had absorbed from some Christian thinking that people aren't born with gay tendencies, that they choose that lifestyle. It was easy to take a strong stand against things that I had absolutely no deep understanding of.

You know what changed me? Relationships. When I found myself with friends and family who were in these situations, the whole thing stopped being abstract theory. Now instead of shaking my fist at some cold concept, I see a face- a soul- that's beautiful and complex. I'm dealing with people God loves, not theory.

I now see that the issues aren't so black and white as I once thought. For instance, I still firmly believe in the sanctity of all life, but I never stopped to think what it would be like for those who are pregnant and are confronted with a difficult decision. Not really. I never considered that there were circumstances so drastically different from my own that abortion might look like a good option. And whatever your stance on homosexuality, it doesn't prevent someone from loving or being loved by God. Period.

So does love look more like a boycott sign or a listening ear?

I'm absolutely certain that we Christians have perpetuated a lot of hurt in the name of being zealous for God, in the name of morality. I've found that even where our understanding of morality is "right", our condemnation belittles humanity. Further, it's not OK for us to ignore people just because we can't find a spot for them in our neat little categories of morality. Jesus certainly didn't, and if we're honest we'll find that none of us really fits into a perfect moral box.

And I know some who read this will say that we can't be "soft" on sin or on things we don't believe are right. There's certainly a time to take a strong stand for righteousness. But here's the thing- being willing to understand or listen to someone else's perspective or story doesn't always mean you have to change what you believe; it also doesn't mean we're responsible for changing what they believe.

Our broken world calls first for love- a genuine love that is willing to peel past the layers of what we disagree with to find the heart of the person inside.

When I was only willing to argue to the death for the issues I find in the Bible, I was missing what the Bible is really about. I was choosing the easy way out, hiding behind theology, rules, and manmade righteousness. To truly be genuine and make an impact on those around us, we simply have to be willing to meet people where they are at without a single ounce of condemnation or judgement. Why is this so hard for us in the church? For me?

THE FINE LINE OF MORALITY

I was recently reading a book by a Christian mother hoping to impart godly wisdom and encouragement to others in the parenting fray. Though I found many of her anecdotes humorous, I bristled at others, such as the story she told about explaining alcohol to her daughter. Having never had a drink herself, the mom described alcohol to her child as a bad tasting drink that makes you act strange. When her daughter inquired why on earth people would drink said bad tasting drink, the mother replied that people drink it as a way to handle different problems in their life.

End of explanation.

I've found this sort of oversimplification to be typical of the conservative Christian mentality. I have no qualms with those who abstain from alcohol or make other strong rules for their family, but there's a danger in over reducing rules of morality. It's easy to explain something you disagree with as being *all* bad, motivated by *only* negative reasons, with *always* unhealthy results. This alcohol advice leaves no room for a glass of wine at the end of the day to unwind, a couple beers over a football game, or heaven forbid a celebratory glass of champagne at a wedding. Are all those people coping with problems?

Like the girl in the story, I also grew up like a sponge, soaking in even the unspoken rules of morality. My parents never actually sat us down and said, "Verily, drinking is wrong, and anyone who drinks is a degenerate", but somehow I still grew up believing it was wrong. Until I was a teen they never had any alcohol in the house, unless you count the vanilla extract, so the concept of "fine in moderation" was never communicated to me. If I went to a friend's house, especially one from church, and saw beers in their fridge I had trouble mentally reconciling their parents' faith status with what appeared to me to be a giant Christian "don't".

Drinking was communicated to me as a black and white morality issue. Though my parents weren't preaching judgmentalism, it was never explained to me till much later that there are gray issues and two people who very much love God can land in two different places. Both sides can easily judge the other, both feeling right, nobody seeing room for grace.

The truth is, I don't believe all drinking is wrong, so it's easy for me to use that as an example of oversimplification. But allow me to use an example of something I draw hard lines about in my own understanding of following God where others see quite differently: I grew up learning that it's biblically inappropriate to "misuse God's name".[1] Fine, most Christians would agree on that. Well for us, that included not saying, "Oh my God". So to this day, that's something I'm strict with my own kids about because in my heart it doesn't sit right.

However, do you know how many godly people I know that use that phrase? (The technical answer is oodles.) So what do I make of that? Was it simply how I was raised? Is the Bible absolutely clear on that point? I don't know. Do I think that all those other people are cavalier and rebellious in their faith? No. Emphatically, no. And perhaps my substitution of "gosh" isn't really fooling "gosh" Himself.

Just as moderation isn't often preached, I find Christian circles often abandon the tension of Biblical ambiguity. While some things in the Bible are straightforward, we can't drop our judgmentalism until we're taught to live in the discomfort of grace.

Maybe some things in the Bible aren't as cut and dry as others. Maybe people's understanding of an application of scripture leads them to a different point-of-view. Perhaps someone falls in love with Jesus as an adult and old habits die hard, or they're simply still learning what God says about different issues. Aren't we all?

I have to find a way to raise my kids confidently in the moral choices our family has settled on between us and God while also teaching them that others, even other Christians, may not take the same approach.

This is a lot messier. It certainly doesn't feel as safe, and the ambiguity can make me feel like I'm watering down God's commands. But if I weren't allowed the freedom to walk in that moral uncertainty, I wouldn't be able to function today as a Christian. If I can't accept other Christians with different viewpoints without judging, I'll miss out on healthy community. If I look to outward actions as signs of someone's spiritual maturity, I become proud and forget that we're all in process.

Being unable to walk in that that tension also prevents us from loving those outside the church well. Seems like it would be hard to love the world if I were always hiding from it or judging it.

Finally, the more I live like I'm the only one with the rules to the game we are playing, the more I start to believe I'm God. And the more I play God the less room I allow for the possibility that God's grace and salvation work in ways that I can't comprehend.

Our very faith is based on a love that chose us in our brokenness. "...God demonstrates his own love for us in this: While we were still sinners, Christ died for us."[2] God didn't wait until we were all "right" to die for us; shouldn't we leave room for Him to show that grace to others we may not agree with? In fact, shouldn't we rejoice in that? Let's embrace a little messy grace because, frankly, we need it too.

PARTLY RIGHT, PARTLY WRONG

One of the most amazing messages I remember of my dad's is that we're all "partly right, partly wrong" people. Though he didn't share this from a pulpit till I was in my twenties, the thought began to permeate my parents' point of view much earlier and shaped me. The concept is so simple, but so freeing and deep at the same time.

The idea forces me into the tight place between the gray areas of what I believe and what you believe. It means that God is speaking to each of us, revealing truths to us at different points. He's always growing us, so we won't wake up this side of heaven having arrived at the fullness of knowledge and truth.[3]

This idea goes hand in hand with walking in moral tension. When we realize that we don't have all the answers, it's easier for us to extend grace and non-judgmentalism when we have disagreements with others. When we admit that maybe God is working out a revelation or truth in someone else's life, we realize we actually need others. We need the perspective and insight and even disagreements from others to help balance us- to keep us seeking and drawing closer to God's heart.

But this extends even to people outside the church. In another of his sermons, my dad challenged my perception that you're either a Christian or a non-Christian and only Christians have spiritual worth to share with the world. My dad drew a long horizontal line across several pages and made vertical marks all along the line to represent different people. He showed how in reality we're all somewhere on that spiritual line in relation to God. Certainly there's a distinction between someone who chooses to accept God and someone who doesn't, but the truth is we're all in process- all on a journey, if you will.

God created us all in His image, which means that the beautiful things of this world that people create, whether music or art or love or family- these are all pieces of God's creativity in us. God may well speak to us through someone who hasn't chosen to follow Him. Where we are on that spiritual line doesn't make us more or less a creation of God, a creation who has something to offer the world.

For me, this has huge implications; sharing my faith ceases to be a one way exchange where I share truth and the other person "converts" to my faith. I don't have to feel like I did something wrong if a good conversation means listening to someone else's faith- listening to their story and not interrupting them every four minutes in an attempt to "fix" them.

It even means it's OK if someone outside of Christianity shares something about their faith or belief that resonates with me- because maybe God gave me a truth through them. I can still hold firmly to Jesus and desire to share His hope with the world without tuning out what the world is saying. In fact, I might be able to share my faith better by listening.

Suddenly my worldview doesn't have to be so cut and dry. It's hard to feel OK with Christianity if I feel like I have the corner on truth and everyone else is floundering in a sea of wrong thought and rebellion. Doesn't it make sense that people can experience God even if they can't put a finger on Him? Doesn't it make sense that God is drawing people to Him right where they are at, in a variety of ways that might look a bit unorthodox to us at times?

Does it really seem fair or possible that only those of us who grew up in the church or memorized just the right amount of scripture or never committed "one of those big sins" have access to God and truth and wisdom? Is it possible that someone with a drastically different background and point of view might actually be able to teach me something about God and his design for life? I don't think I could stick around this faith if I didn't believe in that possibility.

HOLINESS

I used to mostly picture Jesus smiling, maybe with slightly messy brown hair, and wearing a white robe with a blue sash. When the blue sash came into play, I'm not sure, but it's like Jesus' trademark. Almost like the red and white striped "Waldo", you could always spot Jesus in His sash. And I always pictured him with rather Caucasian features, like blue eyes and pale skin, even though the man was clearly of Jewish ethnicity.

Part of the mystery of Jesus as a God-man is that He somehow traded His God appearance to clothe Himself fully in humanity. When the prophet Isaiah spoke of the coming Jesus, he said, "He had no beauty or majesty to attract us to him, nothing in his appearance that we should desire him."[4] He was plain vanilla-- there was nothing even attractive about His looks, much less God-like.

Still, I've sometimes had such a human picture of Jesus that I forget the God part. I forget that God is the I AM, "who is, and who was, and who is to come"[5]. I forget that He is Creator, all-powerful, glorious, beyond comprehension….I forget that He is holy.

But if you want a quick picture of God in His holiness, John gives a glimpse in Revelation 1:13-16. He says Jesus was

> *"dressed in a robe reaching down to his feet and with a golden sash around his chest. The hair on his head was white like wool, as white as snow, and his eyes were like blazing fire. His feet were like bronze glowing in a furnace, and his voice was like the sound of rushing waters. In his right hand he held seven stars, and coming out of his mouth was a sharp, double-edged sword. His face was like the sun shining in all its brilliance."*

I don't know about you, but that's not the Jesus I grew up with- he even traded the blue sash for a golden one. This Jesus is almost frightening- in fact, when John has this vision of Him he's so overcome that he falls down like a dead person. Because Jesus is holy.

Frankly, I don't always want to think about holy God- holy God is a little too bright to look at- He's a little intimidating, a bit too wonderful to grasp. And when I stand in the presence of holy God, I suddenly feel the full weight of my tininess against the magnitude of the One who sustains everything.

Sometimes I don't understand God and His laws- I can't process why He places so much emphasis on certain morality. I can't fathom His judgement or His righteousness. So I want blue-sash Jesus to come and tell me that it doesn't really matter what I do, because He will forgive me and love me anyway.

I don't believe there's a limit to God's forgiveness when we turn to Him, but what I'm really wrestling with is that I don't get to argue with holy God. If God is holy, then even when I don't understand His commands, I need to obey to the fullest I know how, because how can a human argue with divinity? When I'm confronted with a holy God, His holiness eclipses my sense of entitlement and self-justification, eclipses even my questions and doubts. Who can utter anything before holiness?

The word sin has a strange sound to it. Even when I say it, I feel like I'm using an archaic religious concept that doesn't fit into modern society. It's like I'm running around speaking in Shakespearean language and pretending that's totally normal. But while the word may seem a relic, and the concept a bit offensive in our modern culture, if I'm really going to believe in a holy God, I ultimately have to admit that I don't get to decide what's "right" and "wrong".

The Bible may be vague on some areas of morality- but one thing that's never gray is God's holiness. What does that mean for me? It's kind of an anchor, really- I may look around thoroughly perplexed to see that everyone has a different idea of what it means to be moral or good or righteous- but I believe that God is the only one who holds and understands untwisted, untainted truth and righteousness.

And while I have peace of mind that someone actually does have a say on this morality thing, it also means a daily humility on my part. I throw up my hands sometimes and say, "God I don't understand, this isn't going to hurt anyone, why is it off limits?" But I'm pretty sure the world would still be broken if it were run by Carrye's morality. And though everyone else's idea of morality is a bit different from mine, so far none are right enough to fix this world.

If I really believe in who Jesus is, I have to accept all that encompasses. That means I can't take His love and sacrifice and mercy and leave out His holiness, His righteous anger, His God-ness. It also means I respond to His holiness by seeking to follow His heart and accepting His process to make me holy too.[6]

There may be times I want to question His morality, but then who's left to decide? Maybe none of us has the right to be the moral police- maybe none of us is absolutely certain of what's ultimately right. But if holy God exists, do I have any other response but to constantly and humbly defer to Him?

EXPERIMENT #4:

(PART 1) Find a comfortable place to kneel down. Read through Bible passages that declare God's holiness and power (Revelation 4:8-11, Job 38, 1Timothy 6:15-16) Or listen to songs like "Revelation Song" by Kari Jobe, or "The Stand" by Hillsong, or "Your Great Name" by Natalie Grant. (These are suggestions- feel free to play songs you most resonate with.) The posture of kneeling or bowing sometimes helps us to physically acknowledge who God is. Verbally acknowledge His holiness and that you accept His Lordship in your life. Consider your smallness and brokenness in relation to who He is.

(PART 2) Instead of dwelling on your smallness and brokenness to the point of guilt and despair, now consider the amazing love of the Father who made a way for you to approach His throne with confidence (Hebrews 4:16). Relish the fact that you're covered by Jesus' holiness, that God has removed your sins "as far as the east is from the west" (Psalm 103:12). Take a moment to just dwell on how great His love for us is, that covers over our worst sins. Write any thoughts that come to you during this time.

5
GRAY EVANGELISM

WITNESSING

I was under the delusion that my first practice with "witnessing", or sharing my faith, was with my stuffed animals in my crib. I'm not sure how I thought that went down. Maybe Mr. Bear wasn't sharing his toys with Fuzzy Fox so I sat him down to explain how his little stuffed heart needed Jesus.

My mom says that, in reality, my first practice sharing my faith was in my *sister's* crib talking about God with a few girls from playgroup. But my first true recollection of trying to defend God and share my faith was around age five with a friend in my mom's home day care.

My friend told me quite emphatically that she loved Power Rangers *the best*. I asked her if she was *sure* she loved Power Rangers the best, or if she loved God the best. I was graciously allowing her to reconsider her sacrilege. She replied that she loved them both the best, and I assured her that this was theologically unsound. She couldn't love them both the best, and the only appropriate biblically appropriate answer to my question was "God".

My poor mom tried to explain a little evangelical sensitivity to me after that.

Since then I'm not sure the sharing of my faith has much improved. I'm not so blunt and headstrong as before- in fact I've felt rather awkward sharing my faith over the years. Once I tried sticking a spiritual note in a helium balloon in the hopes that it would divinely lose air at just the right moment and land near someone who needed God. And who hopefully was in the habit of ripping open stray balloons. (It's OK to laugh.)

I wrote a similar "Jesus loves you" note to put in a desk my parents were getting rid of on the side of the road. *"You thought you were just getting a piece of furniture for your office but I bet you didn't expect to get Jesus too! Hehe!"*

Otherwise, often my best evangelism technique was to simply hope someone asked what my Dad did for a living, or subtly work the word "church" into our conversation. Easy does it. Once a girl from church brought her friend over to me and actually asked me point blank to explain what it meant to be a Christian, and I was instantly nervous. I felt unqualified and told them maybe they should ask one of the parents.

I grew up with this overwhelming sense that I needed to be showing Christ to everyone at all times. Aside from just telling people about God, some Christians suggested that we should live squeaky clean lives so that people would know we were really different, that our faith was genuine. Some said we would "ruin our testimony" (translation: kill our chance to share our faith), if someone caught us doing something they thought was wrong.

That's kind of a crazy burden to carry- to think that any Joe Schmo might see a snapshot of my life and think, *"Well gee, she just yelled at her kids, I find myself seriously doubting her whole schtick about believing in God."*

In reality, if Christianity depended on anyone other than Jesus being perfect, it would cease to be Christianity. 1 Peter 2:12 says that we should "live such good lives among the pagans that, though they accuse you of doing wrong, they may see your good deeds and glorify God", but there's a difference between living a life that shows the grace of God and living out of our own strength to appear perfect to others.

And I can't help wondering if the phrase "live such good lives" has perhaps more to do with what we SHOULD do than what we SHOULDN'T do. Will people be curious about our lives if we live sacrificially, if they see us loving others when it doesn't make sense? Will they wonder what makes us different if they see that we aren't caught up in the rat race? Or imagine what impact I'd make if I were more concerned with genuinely listening and paying attention to other people than worrying about what mistakes they might see me make?

Beyond that, I've been paralyzed by feeling that every encounter I have with anyone anywhere has to tangibly further them towards God. Everyone? Let's take the guy working in the tollbooth: I mean, how much do I really believe in the power of a Christian smile? Because aside from coins, that's about all I've got to give him. The Starbucks barista at the drive-thru? Unless I'm dedicated to coming in *really* regularly, my interaction with her is more likely to be about my sugar-free latte than her latest thoughts on the Trinity.

Often going out of my way to be friendly to someone is the most I can do. Yes, God wants us to show kindness and respect to strangers we encounter, but the feeling that I'm personally responsible for every soul I run into is not only counterproductive, but unbiblical.

The weight of witnessing can also prevent us from being authentic. Sometimes I feel like I'm not even sure how to be myself with others- or if it's even OK to be myself- because what if my real self is actually a bit sacrilegious? Or what if I'm coming across too self-righteous? I know I should look "different" but isn't that difference supposed to be something Christ does in me, instead of me trying really hard to be what I think a Christian should be?

I can't muster up godliness any more than I can will my eyes to change from blue to brown. I'm still growing comfortable in who I am, who God made me to be, but I'm beginning to realize that I don't have to be more than my broken self to share God with people. In fact, I wonder if all my striving is really me trying to share Christ without Christ. Perhaps my greatest purpose is simply to be still and love God first, and sharing my faith will flow out of walking with Him.

IF YOU DIED TONIGHT

"Because, who knows, what if you get hit by a car on the way home tonight?"

Those words were spoken by a youth pastor at a Southern youth group meeting of maybe 35 teens, but it could have been any church. We had the cool music, the technology and big screen, videos and drama- all to connect with the most people. The youth pastor went up and shared a short message which included a presentation of the gospel- how to invite Jesus to be a part of your life. He finished with the question,

"If you died tonight, do you know what would happen to you?"

The question was clearly meant to drive home both the gravity and urgency of knowing the eternal state of our souls. The message, spoken from countless church platforms, was essentially: *choose now whether you plan to spend eternity in heaven or hell because once you die you don't get to choose.*

While certainly attention grabbing, I don't think this message is best.

First, for those growing up in the church hearing this over and over, this tactic gives the impression that we're in the business of converting people as quickly as possible. If we don't share our faith strongly enough, or if someone doesn't want to accept our faith, does that mean we are forever responsible for missing an opportunity? It seems to me that someone hearing about God and accepting Him is often a process- not something that need always be instantaneous. Not to mention the Spirit has kind of an important role in drawing people as well- we're just a piece of the process. Talk about taking some pressure off.

The second flaw I see in this method of presenting the gospel is that it's so fear based. So what if someone does choose to accept Christ because they don't want to go home tonight afraid of eternal death? Where does that person go from there? How long will it take them to learn that life begins now- that hope begins here on earth no matter what the circumstance? Will they consider their soul eternally cared for and never search out intimacy with Christ? Will they even rest assured of their salvation or will they constantly be looking over their shoulder, re-doing their prayer to God, hoping all the time that they really are going to heaven?

A respectful fear of God is one thing- an awe, recognizing our smallness in His presence. But otherwise, I'm not sure fear is the best route to understanding the vastness of God's love and his heart for us.

TOILETS & TRACTS

When I was sixteen years old I went to Costa Rica on my first missions trip out of the country. Upon our arrival at the church that hosted us, the staff said, "do not put toilet paper in the toilet." Come again? The sanitary system was too weak, and the paper would get clogged I guess- the reason is a little fuzzy for me. But what's crystal clear in my memory is that all the toilet paper went in a little waste basket *next* to the toilet.

This was a small, if not unusual, sacrifice in leaving America behind- certainly less troubling than cold showers that occasionally hosted large cockroaches. Seriously, I stood under a trickle of water cleaning myself, one eye on the soap, one eye staring down the roaches. At some point I realized, with horror and trepidation, that I was going to have to close my eyes to wash my hair. I imagined the roaches were waiting for this exact moment to suddenly shift closer. They told us to bring flip flops to wear in the shower, but I thought that was for general sanitation, not warding off large insects.

Anyway, the toilet paper in the trash was gross, but nothing I couldn't handle...until under force of habit I dropped my toilet paper wad right into the latrine. Egads. What should I do? I suppose a normal person would have left the thing alone, flushed, and prayed to God the whole Costa Rican public waste system didn't back up. I either couldn't bear the thought of causing the certain failure of said system, or didn't believe that God cared to spend his time taking care of plumbing issues. Either way, in my panic I found myself fishing disgusting, clingy, wet toilet paper out of the toilet to drop it in the nearby trash.

Despite the awkward moment, traveling to Costa Rica on a missions trip was the culmination of a dream for me. As a child, I remember a woman in my church returning from a trip to Mexico, sharing pictures and stories about the children and people she encountered in villages. She talked about how she laughed with the kids in the orphanage, joking with the boys with one of the few Spanish words she knew, "fuerte" (strong), as they would flex their arms to show off their muscles.

This woman and other missionaries who stayed in our home from time to time stirred in me the desire to travel to another country for myself one day. So at age sixteen I was ecstatic to be asked to go with a mother/daughter team to Central America where I could use my budding Spanish skills.

I needed around $1500 for the trip and I remember thinking that this was the first time I, and not my parents, had to directly trust God to provide for myself financially. I sent out support letters and babysat like crazy and now have several journal entries to remind me how God brought in money from so many generous sponsors. I was ready to go on this trip- to make a difference in the world- to experience another culture and language.

Once in Costa Rica, I was part of a small team that travelled to schools and public areas performing a couple of funny skits followed by a more serious drama that portrayed the gospel message. We had translators that went around with us to help us talk to people afterwards, and we had some tracts printed in Spanish to pass out to anyone and everyone.

One memorable day, we ended up in a sort of village green. We did our skit in the pouring rain and talked with people under a gazebo. I remember feeling discouraged about the rain, but even more disheartened as I watched a couple of teenage boys discard the tracts that we had just given them into a nearby fountain. They showed about as much contempt or disdain for those tracts as I showed for the used toilet paper I had thrown in the trash can by the toilet.

Looking back I question the spiritual impact we made on the people in Costa Rica. I certainly experienced a new culture, and I felt a greater understanding of the global church. At a local church service I fell in love with multiple cultures and tongues worshipping God together in the same place. That was a beautiful picture of heaven, and it was a genuine moment. The people that housed us and fed us were genuine- the fried *platanos* and platters of chicken, rice and beans were genuine. But I don't feel that we offered much that was genuine to the Costa Ricans that we met.

Because to be genuine, especially where there's a language barrier and a week time limit, you have to physically DO something to show the love of Christ. Our drama may have connected with a select few, but it was far off from the situations that the people were in. It didn't connect with the old men smoking on the park benches saying "I love you" in thick Spanish accents to the girls in our group.

What tangible hope did we offer to women or men hurrying down the streets- what evidence of Christ's love did we show to the people happily enjoying a festival in a park? If I'm brutally, painstakingly honest, how much more was I offering than a neatly pre-packaged, shrink-wrapped, mass produced gospel message?

I've since gone on two short term trips to the tiny Central American country of Belize. On both trips our group helped to plan and execute a VBS for the children, and we did some minor construction work for the local church. Honestly, I still felt that there was a disconnect with some of the children, and I fear we didn't impact the area around the church as much as we could. That's a general downfall of short term missions trips- we can't fully connect and engage people because we aren't living among them regularly, sharing their ongoing joys and concerns.

But at least on that trip we worshipped in the same place for a week, and so when we tithed to the church there it was not with strangers but with those who knew our hearts, shared meals, and worked alongside of us. We left behind something tangible- we put in toil and sweat- a sacrifice that wasn't worth it unless we believed what we were sharing about Christ.

Today, I'm skeptical of certain types of short term missions trips. I fear that we send out our teens and adult leaders with a smile, teach them to say "Jesus loves you" in the necessary language, and plan out gospel messages that are true but ring hollow with those we encounter. If we merely show up to fix people with a message, we're emptying the gospel of the love and passion and action of Christ.

But when God-followers go and build homes for those in poverty, or provide clothing and food for the underdressed and malnourished, the message of Christ is backed by the truth of action. It's the religion that God finds pure and faultless.[1] That's not something people want to throw away.

GET TO THE PRAYING HANDS

On one mission trip to Belize our group joined up with other churches to serve the local community. One of our first days there, a group leader from another organization sat us all down in our hotel to give us a presentation on how to have a conversation with just about anyone. The presentation wasn't all bad, especially for those who struggle to talk with people they've just met.

The idea was to take a series of images and associate each with a topic of conversation. So you might picture a house to trigger you to ask about where someone lives, or a goal post to remind you to ask them about their hobbies and recreation. It got a bit confusing as there were about fifteen images that we were supposed to imagine precariously stacked on top of each other, and the goal was to move from the bottom of the pile of images to the top. At the very top I remember there were praying hands, obviously symbolizing praying with someone, possibly even leading them to accept God.

After the presentation we were supposed to pair off with someone we didn't know well and practice going through the steps of conversation, ending in prayer. Except this was a strategy drill, so we were timed- maybe five minutes at first. Each partner was trying to ask questions and genuinely listen, all the while counting through the bizarre images yet to get through and feeling panicked because the praying hands were so far away. Then we had to switch partners and go even faster. It felt a little like this:

"Hi, your name is...yes, I'm Carrye...you live in Albuquerque? That must be nice. Uh, crud, I think we're supposed to be talking about hobbies now. You first. You have how many pug dogs?! Fifteen? I....wait, did we skip your occupation? Hm, why did you decide to work in the taxidermy field...? Oops, hold that thought, that's the 15 second warning we'd better skip straight to prayer. Jesus, thank you for this nice Pug-loving, taxidermist from Albuquerque. Amen."

Whenever Christians put forth strategies or tools for reaching out to people, I think there has to be a careful consideration that we aren't pushing the wrong message. I understand the point of this tool was to help us specifically on the short term mission trip when we might meet people that we'd only get one chance to ever speak with. But even there, I still fear there's such a push to get us to talk with people with the end goal of prayer and conversion in mind. It's an unhealthy expectation, and it can prevent us from truly wanting to know someone for themselves, with no ulterior motive.

While we can learn a formula to aid our interactions with people, neither people nor salvation is formulaic. We are absolutely commanded to share our faith, and should always be ready to give an answer for the hope we have in God.[2] But God's part in the process is actually bigger than ours, and He doesn't have a one-size-fits-all format for reaching people.

TESTIMONY

In Christian circles, "testimony" is a key word in evangelism. I always thought of it as your conversion story- how you came to accept Christ and how that decision changed your life- a "before and after" if you will.

Before I became a Christian I _____ (fill in the blank with all the heinous things you once did or your miserable state of depravity), *and now that I'm a Christian I* _____ (fill in the blank with experiences of joy, freedom, and the general rosiness of life).

Our church would have baptism services where those who've chosen to follow Christ are immersed in water as a symbol of their new life, and people would publicly share their testimony. I would listen to stories of people who'd lived it rough- maybe there was addiction, or a string of harmful relationships, or some other massive brokenness in their lives. But the stories always seemed to end with the person somehow fixed and in a better place because of Christ in their lives. I figured if you shared one of *those* stories with someone who didn't know God, you would be an evangelistic super-star.

But here was my dilemma: I grew up being taught about God since infancy, and my five year old "conversion" in my living room was fairly lackluster. There was no weeping in repentance. I wasn't singing praises to God. It was a positive moment, as I recall, but there was no sudden feeling that I was a new person. I actually re-prayed "the prayer" at least once hoping I got it right the first time. And I honestly grew up thinking that my testimony was kind of crappy.

How am I supposed to lead someone to God with a story like, "I was a pretty good kid, but when my mom asked me about accepting Jesus to lead my life, I thought it was a solid plan. Plus that heaven thing sounded pretty appealing. After that…(dramatic pause)…I was still a pretty good kid."

I thought it was a shame that my story didn't go something like this:

"I was a hopelessly lost kid before I met God. I mean, I was daily cursing out my parents, always slinging pointy rocks at the preschoolers, and was the only kindergartener hard-core enough to be invited to join the first grader's gang. But once I found God, man, it was sunshine from there- my parents stopped asking God where they'd gone wrong, I sent care packages to all the preschoolers I'd injured, and I've been witnessing to the stone-cold first graders in that gang ever since."

It took me a very long time to realize that your testimony doesn't have to be the part of your story where you first find God, or accept Him. It doesn't have to be about a massive change in your life. Your testimony is any story of you experiencing God in an intimate way, any event that shaped how you view God, how you relate to Him, or how you find Him in even the everyday.

How freeing to know that I can share my faith without having to sit someone down and tell them a forced spiritual story about accepting God; I can weave my honest faith into stories in regular conversations as friends ask about my life. I don't have to plot or scheme at what point in my relationship with someone I need to share my end all testimony, because as we relate to people we will naturally find places to share how Christ intersects our daily humanity.

I've also become increasingly wary of testimonies that sound like a before and after. People want to share and celebrate all the wonderful changes God has made in their lives since they've turned to Him- and they should!

But I've struggled because accepting God isn't the end of our process to being made holy. In many ways, we continue to accept God *daily* the rest of our lives. It's why Jesus says we must take our cross up daily[3] and ask Him for our daily bread.[4] God has redeemed us once for all, but He knows our hearts will have to choose to follow and trust Him over and over.

I realized how disillusioning it is to assume that once you have Christ all your problems are fixed. I do believe that to have Christ is to have hope for this life and beyond, but that doesn't make me a perfect person. It doesn't mean that I won't struggle with doubt, fear, anger, depression, lust, pride, selfishness or personal vices. I love to hear people share stories that rejoice in what God has done for them without glossing over the broken struggle that remains, the jagged pieces of our messy world.

Sharing our stories with the world is absolutely vital in sharing our faith. I'm not suggesting we do away with testimonies altogether, but I do think we should be thoughtful in how we talk about sharing our faith. Maybe especially for those who grow up in the church, we need to hear the message that your story of following Christ doesn't have to be summarized in a few spiritually positive sentences, nor does it have to be void of ongoing struggle. We need to feel free to tell our story as it really is- because the world doesn't need a polished, dramatic story; it needs your honest one.

EXPERIMENT #5

Think about your life and the people you've shared your faith with. How does evangelism make you feel? If you're like me, you may feel ashamed that you haven't shared your faith story more often. Or, you might be someone who has shared your faith often, but you've struggled with whether your approach honors God. Ask God to identify one thing about how you share you faith that you can improve in. (If you're stuck try praying about one of these: Listening better to others, being more sensitive to God's Spirit, arguing less, being more confident in sharing the story God's given you, worrying less about having a "perfect" testimony, genuinely loving those you are sharing with, trusting the Spirit's role in speaking to people, etc.) Just pick one thing. The next time you encounter someone and feel impressed to share part of your faith story, trust God to help you with that piece of evangelism He wants to grow you in.

6
GRAY EXPECTATIONS

MISSING OUT ON THE PARTY

Have you ever felt like you were the one person in a room that didn't belong there? This happened for me during a worship night over my short stay in Costa Rica. A leader spoke briefly, then there was worship music playing and the next thing I knew it seemed like everyone was either raising their hands in praise, or sobbing or generally being overcome by God's presence.

I tried. I really did. I closed my eyes. I focused. I prayed. For the amount I was concentrating on trying to experience God, I should have been levitating or at least glowing in holy radiance. But I couldn't seem to get to the spiritual state everyone else had made it to, and I felt like I was missing out. Worse, I felt like something must be wrong with me. And that's certainly not the only time in my life I've felt that I'm coming up short spiritually in a church setting, or even in my own quiet prayer time at home.

Sometimes I have an emotional connection with God- sometimes worship brings me to tears. Often when a song resonates with my life I feel like raising my hands in abandon, almost as though I'm offering my whole self to God in a physical way. But there are other times I feel dry- I don't believe in God less, but I struggle to feel His presence. My head or my circumstances get in the way. Or maybe God's presence isn't always emotional- maybe sometimes He's just as present in the struggle to find Him, in the numb feelings or the humanness of my attempts to follow.

I don't know that I can expect my feelings with God to be different than with my own husband. In my head I might always know that I love him, but if I based our relationship on my feelings or emotions alone, I could easily assume our love was not constant, not genuine. In reality, I wonder if a sacrifice of love for my spouse when I don't feel like it actually speaks more about my commitment to him than any amount of emotional or romantic love. Likewise, maybe my frail attempts to trust God when I'm struggling to feel His love are especially beautiful to Him.

Faith is not a constant string of good feelings; to think we should always be in some euphoric state of oneness with God is to set ourselves up for painfully unattainable expectations. Deep down the dry times remind us that even our relationship with God was broken in the garden of Eden. We long for a time when we can continuously know and experience God without doubt, without needing faith at all.

Romans 8:24 says, "But hope that is seen is no hope at all. Who hopes for what they already have?" If we already had a relationship with God that filled us completely and never left us questioning- if we'd already attained freedom from all the baggage and pain of this life- would we still be longing for what is to come?

At times others around us might seem like they're closer to God- we might feel like we're missing out on an elusive party that everyone got invited to but us. Watching how God works in other people and how they interact with Him can be a very positive thing, helping us realize the different ways God shows Himself to us. However, I can't try to determine my spiritual state by comparing myself with Christians around me.

When everyone seems to be full of God but me, I don't need to feel foolish or wrong. I must believe God sees my heart and would rather an honest acknowledgement of struggle than a pretense of praise.

FAITH GROWS IN A HARD PLACE

I had my first child, a sweet tiny girl, at age 22. During my pregnancy I was blindsided by a diagnosis of gestational diabetes. It's not a very common complication, and those that have it can normally control it with diet and exercise. For some reason I wasn't able to control it with either; instead I had to take insulin shots. It was a stressful time but I told myself that I just had to hold on for a few more months- once I had the baby, the hormones that made my body resistant to my insulin would be gone, and with them my diabetic symptoms. Apparently not.

To this day I'm not sure what triggered diabetes in my body, but just a few months after my daughter was born I knew something was wrong. I was increasingly nauseous (not pregnant again, I checked!) and my vision was daily getting fuzzier. I didn't want to think that it could be diabetes, but I decided to check my blood sugar with the glucose monitor I still had from the pregnancy. My levels were upwards of 400 mg/dL! If this isn't shocking news, you should know that a normal person's blood glucose ranges closer to 100 mg/dL. The endocrinologist ran blood work that confirmed: I was diagnosed with late onset type 1 diabetes, which meant that I would be insulin dependent the rest of my life.

The rest of my life, and all that entailed, didn't sink in right away. When the doctor called to tell me the blood work results I could tell he was disheartened about giving me bad news. Somehow I felt like I was the calm one during the conversation, politely and matter-of-factly accepting the news as though I'd known it would happen my whole life. But the reality of living with diabetes eventually smacked me pretty hard in the face.

In the last six years I've had scary low blood sugar episodes, unexplainable high levels, and insurance companies that don't send my life-preserving supplies on time. Fear has crept into certain activities that I once would have done without a thought, and I live with a sense of vulnerability that I can't fully express. It's been a truly life-altering diagnosis.

From the outside it often appears that I live a normal life, and in many ways I do. I'm extremely grateful for the medical advances that allow me to exist in relative normalcy. But there's not a day that goes by that I'm not tethered to my insulin pump, that I don't fear where my glucose levels are at, that I don't have to think about what I eat or how just playing in the yard with my kids might affect me.

But a truly defining moment in my life came when I told God that for whatever struggle and pain and fear I've been through, I'm grateful that it has brought me to a place of *desperation* for Him. Because there's something about my middle-class American culture that had made it so hard for me to *need* God in any deep place. I thanked Him for food, but we'd never gone without food. I thanked Him for a house, but we always had a place to sleep. I never feared for my life or my daily needs so even though I knew I "needed" God, I hadn't had much of a chance to test that.

The desperation of diabetes not only brought me to a closer intimacy with Christ than I'd ever known, it also brought me to the place of seeing His hand of blessing when I was legitimately powerless to change my situation.

There was one time when our insurance changed and I expected my insulin pump to be covered, only to find out it was being denied. When I made some phone calls to challenge that, I was told by not only the insurance company but also people from my pump manufacturer and pharmacy that others had tried in the past to get this pump covered, and my chance of success was bleak. Somehow I heard that grim report and didn't freak out. Looking back I had an absurd amount of peace because I thought to myself that my God is in the habit of doing the undoable and so I wasn't ready to take no for an answer.

Believe it or not, after the string of tedious phone calls that got me nowhere, the insurance company finally agreed to cover my pump because I sent a complaint to a random email address I found on the insurance website. Seriously, how does that make sense? Less than a week after sending my email I had someone calling ME to sort things out and help me get my pump covered. That was one of my defining "God" moments, when I knew that God is so much bigger than I act like He is. Apparently He doesn't need my worry or my striving to accomplish amazing things. I've come to love verses in the Bible like Isaiah 59:1: "Surely the arm of the Lord is not too short to save, nor his ear too dull to hear."

God met me in my crisis- He showed up where my human strength ended.

Today, for all the intimacy I've had with God through the diabetes, I've not been in a great place with it. And honestly, more often than praying that God will use it in my life for His glory, I simply pray that He will heal me and take it away. I've gone through months of anxiety and fear that have kept me from really living my fullest life, and there are days that it overtakes my thoughts.

Even though diabetes has brought me closer to God, it's still not something I'd wish on my friends or, heaven forbid, my kids. But it reminds me as I watch my kids' lives that they may grow the most from the things I most want to protect them from. Diabetes is one of the ways I experience a broken world, and my kids will have their own piece of brokenness to carry. I can't keep them from all the heartache, and frankly I shouldn't try to because sometimes only in loss and pain do we ask the honest questions that clarify our faith.

So the questions flow: Can I believe in a good God when my circumstances are disappointing? Is it possible that Jesus Himself can become so precious to me as to eclipse my problems? Is my faith based on what I think God should do for me, or on who He is? Can God accept my human belief in the midst of pain, anger or doubts? And can I accept that trials might actually give me a better perspective on what life is really about- that they might actually help me find more of God? My answer is becoming more and more a confident, "yes".

PRAYER

Once, in a Christian book store, I roamed to a tiny corner in the kid's section with a video playing on a pintsized TV. There were inviting bean bag chairs to boot, so I sat down to watch a talking stuffed bear tell a little boy how to pray. The boy, maybe eight years old, was clearly brand new to talking to God and was anxious to do it "right". As he wrapped up his novice prayer attempt, he asked "Prayer Bear" how he did. Did he do the prayer the way he was supposed to?

Prayer Bear, though trying to be encouraging, gently corrected the boy: "No, we say, 'In Jesus' Name, Amen.'" As if that were the only way to end a prayer, ever. As if somehow every word prayed up to that point was null and void without the magic ending. There's power in Jesus' name, but we don't grasp that concept through rote.

I struggled then, as I do now, with the idea that prayer need be formulaic- as though saying certain words in a certain order allows us to be better heard by God. I remember growing up that I'd get frustrated sometimes with how to pray to God. I'd read the "Lord's Prayer"[1] and knew I was supposed to come to God not just with requests, but also with thanksgiving and reverence for who He is.[2] I'd also read that "God is in heaven and you are on earth, so let your words be few."[3]

Sometimes I would come to God with anger or hurt and I'd start to pray and feel like I was doing it wrong. Was I was saying too much, or praying an inappropriate ratio of venting, requests, thanksgiving and praise? (Is it supposed to be a 20/20/30/30 thing? Is venting even allowed?) And at times other people make it seem like prayer is just this blessing machine. Don't tell anyone I said this, but I actually get irritated sometimes at people's "success" stories and I want to yell, "God doesn't always work that way, you know! He doesn't always give you what you ask for!"

Prayer is something we grow in, just as we grow in depth of conversation with good friends. Yes, there are ways we can honor God with a reverent silence before Him, and there are times to come before Him to simply acknowledge His greatness or thank Him for His goodness. But I realized that my feeling of praying "wrong" made me simply not want to pray, and I don't believe that is God's heart.

Besides, if you spend any time at all in the Psalms you'll find alarmingly raw, honest outpourings to God. To borrow from my favorite Christian comedian (of course I have one!), Mark Lowry, the Psalms make it seem like David may well have been on Prozac; he bounces from heartfelt, poetic praise to statements about how God seems to have utterly abandoned him. And I got to thinking, if this David is a man after God's own heart and *his* prayers were so blunt and human, perhaps it's OK if mine are too.

Aside from learning to be honest in prayer, I'm also seeking to gain a better understanding of the purpose of prayer. If I have a wrong expectation of what prayer is and does, I can easily become bitter or disillusioned with God. Understanding more about prayer requires me to ask some tough questions.

Why does God seemingly answer some prayers and not others? Are prayers answered in proportion to how much faith someone has? God clearly cannot give everyone what they ask for, or He would become a genie rather than God. But then why should we pray if God may not respond? And if prayer is supposed to be my communication with God, why does He seem so painfully far away at times? If I don't hear from Him audibly, how do I know He's there leading me?

Sometimes prayer feels like an elaborate chemistry experiment where everyone is using the same chemicals but getting different results.

I've experienced prayer in different ways throughout my life. Most days I pray several short "help me" or "help them" prayers whenever chaos strikes. I might pray for an immediate diabetic issue, for quick patience with my children, that I could *please* find a parking space, or for a friend that I don't know how to help. Even though these are snippet prayers without much focus, they help me to acknowledge God throughout the day and are my conscious way of trying to turn to Him when I'm weak.

Sometimes if I'm struggling to feel God's presence in the midst of difficulty, I will stop wherever I am and tell God that I don't feel OK- that I need Him to DO something. The more desperate I am the more honest and bold I tend to be. God doesn't always answer right away (or at all sometimes) but in those heart-pouring moments I force myself to wrestle with my God- to ask myself again if my faith in Him is really based on who He is or on my circumstances.

Other times, I carve out specific time when I can be alone with God for a while, to really focus on praying and listening. I might pray for God's direction or that He will fulfill a desire of my heart. I try to make time for thanking Him or praising Him while listening to music. And I try to listen. I've never heard God's voice audibly, but I've heard His thoughts playing through my head, often in some form of a Bible verse. There are times I believe God has lead me to read a Bible verse that speaks so directly into my heart. Other times He will overwhelm me with a fresh peace or understanding of who He is or His sacrifice for me.

I've grown to find that I'm actually quite fond of being in the presence of Jesus this way, that I miss Him when I haven't made time for Him. I know God wants me to bring Him everything- whether praise or fears or questions or requests. I'm learning to be OK when God doesn't answer as I want. Releasing God from the expectation that He will fix all my problems doesn't mean I'm making excuses for Him, it means I'm accepting His God-ness. That means sometimes I'll feel disappointed. But every time I'm with Him I know that He's doing something in me- peeling away some layer of selfishness, changing my heart, or simply giving me joy.

One of my favorite verses now is Psalm 37:4: "Take delight in the Lord, and he will give you the desires of your heart." Once I may have thought that God was saying "Love me and I'll give you anything you want!" But I've learned that, in reality, when I delight myself in Him- seeking His applause and finding His presence- He gives me first and foremost Himself. And there's really nothing better than knowing my Maker. If He is my greatest desire, every other request or fear or want becomes a bit dim in His light. Beyond that, as we humble ourselves before Him in prayer, He gives us His desires, bit by bit. What a beautiful and powerful thing when we want what God wants.

So what is my expectation of prayer? I expect that I will ask God a million more times for things that He won't give, but that He wants to give good things and I must keep asking and honoring Him with my faith. I expect that prayer will fulfill me and perplex me. I expect that God hears though I can't always hear Him. And I expect that prayer will continue to lead me closer to God's heart, and deeper into His presence even when I can't understand Him.

THE LESSON OF JOB & ZEKE

There are a lot of really cool promises in the Bible that we all like to stake claim to. We'll all take a piece of "in all things God works for the good of those who love him",[4] and certainly we believe "God will meet all your needs according to the riches of his glory in Christ Jesus".[5] Or how about Romans 8:36, "No, in all these things we are more than conquerors through him who loved us."

But sometimes we like to take the pleasant, glowing verses out of context, or just leave out the less attractive places in the Bible altogether. For instance, have we ever supposed that God working ALL things for our good probably means he is using the hard stuff too? Have we pondered whether God meeting "all our needs" is referring possibly to something beyond just our physical needs? Dare we read the verses that precede Romans 8:36 that mention WHAT things we are more than conquerors in? (Hardship, persecution and nakedness, to name a few.) Adversity doesn't negate God's promises, but it certainly forces us to confront our faith with a different perspective.

Ezekiel and Job are two Bible characters whose lives perplex me and upturn my simple view of God's blessings. Ezekiel was one of God's prophets to Israel after they stopped obeying God- again. Like a father disciplining His children, God used Zeke to tell the Israelites what consequences would come if they didn't return to Him. But nobody likes to hear about consequences so Zeke wasn't all that popular. Not only that, God made him do elaborate and uncomfortable demonstrations as a sign to the Israelites. For instance, one time God told Ezekiel to lie on his side for over a year, using human feces for cooking fuel.[6]

That seems a bit extreme, even for a good cause. But that wasn't the worst living metaphor he went through. No. I actually cried when I read Ezekiel 24:16, where God told Ezekiel that (A) He was going to take his wife from him and (B) that Ezekiel wasn't supposed to mourn her death.

What?!

I could maybe justify this if God was going to use the death of Ezekiel's wife to save a million others from dying. Or was He going to bring her back to life after taking her to demonstrate His power? NO! It turns out the whole thing was just another object lesson to the stubborn Israelites-

and they still didn't listen. Our guy Zeke gave up everything to follow God, why would God take away more?

And you've probably heard of Job; aside from Jesus he's kind of the Bible's poster boy for suffering. His story shows the behind-the-scenes in the Spiritual world. So you have Satan telling God he's been looking for someone to test, and God says, "Have you tried Job- he's my man- he's as righteous as they come." Satan says, "Yeah, yeah. That's because you gave him a charmed life- no wonder he praises you."

So God tells Satan that, short of killing Job, he has free reign to do what he wants with him. Satan wastes no time- first he takes Job's children all in one fell swoop- then his cattle- his wealth- and finally inflicts him with horrible sores all over his entire body. Job's own wife tells him to "curse God and die".[7] Somehow he never curses God, but he does question God. He wonders where his justice is and asks for the reason for his suffering.

God's "answer" to Job gives the only real answer I have for Ezekiel as well. God says, "Where were you when I laid the earth's foundation"[8]; "Have you ever given orders to the morning, or shown the dawn its place"[9]; "Does the eagle soar at your command and build its nest on high?".[10] There are four full chapters of God reminding Job of who He is- all-knowing Creator, holy God.

He basically tells Job, "You're not the master story teller here. You won't fully understand because you're a piece of creation and you can never comprehend the vastness of my power, authority and wisdom."

Job is completely humbled. He says, "Surely I spoke of things I did not understand, things too wonderful for me to know."[11] Of course, in the end, God returns Job's wealth and gives him more children as a blessing. But Zeke never gets his wife back, nor does he get to see the fruit of his prophecies. Does God's answer remain sufficient when we aren't blessed abundantly in this life, at least not in the way we'd hoped?

Author Donald Miller first impressed on me the idea of seeing God as writer of my story, but moreover that my piece of the story is part of His own grand narrative throughout history. The story is about Him. There was a shift in my expectations of God when I began acknowledging that He's the storyteller AND the main character; I will always be part of the supporting cast.

I'm human, made of dust, and though I know everyone dies eventually, I tend to act like maybe I'm the exception. If the story really were about me I would have a right to be angry with God for giving me anything less than exactly what I want. But Job and Ezekiel remind me that the story is far from my own, and to acknowledge that requires a willingness to accept the plotline that is my life.

It sounds a bit harsh- especially when I grew up thinking that, on some level, Jesus wanted to keep me safe, to make my life thrive and be blessed. That's the promise of "good Christianity", right? But God's answer to Job is His answer to me- and what can I say to such a Creator even if my life isn't what I thought it should be?

Besides, I have more promises to stand on than even Job and Zeke did: I have Jesus' sacrifice. I have knowledge of this Jesus who literally went through hell and back to restore life to His creation- to me. And He did it all "for the joy set before him"[12] because "God so loved the world."[13] If my arguments feel paper thin against the answer of my Creator, how could they stand at all against the love of Creator *and* Savior?

The hurt and disappointment may remain, the questions may linger, but one question eventually eclipses the others: "What right do I have to tell the God who made me and died for me that He can't write His own story through me?" When honoring God's story becomes my expectation, I can learn to be less frustrated and perplexed by events that aren't going my way. Further, as I come to feel Christ's love more fully, how could I possibly have another response than submission to Him? Is there any better way to say "I love you" back to my Maker?

EXPERIMENT #6

Part of experiencing the full life God wants means honestly giving Him our greatest disappointments, hurts, and fears. We have to get to a place where WHO God is outweighs the WHATS of our lives. I won't pretend this is easy, and there isn't a formula for getting there. But if we want to get to know someone better, sometimes asking a question is the best place to start. This week, tell God that you want to know Him better. Ask Him to show you through His Word something about Himself- part of who He is- that will meet you wherever you are at. Read the following verses and pray them for yourself this week:

Ephesians 1:17-19: "I keep asking that the God of our Lord Jesus Christ, the glorious Father, may give you the Spirit of wisdom and revelation, so that you may know him better. I pray that the eyes of your heart may be enlightened in order that you may know the hope to which he has called you, the riches of his glorious inheritance in his holy people, and his incomparably great power for us who believe."

7
GRAY WALK

THE WEIGHT OF "SHOULD"

I can't say how much is my personality and how much is my Christian upbringing, but I've spent a lot of my life trying to do only what I "should" do. Perhaps my belief in moral absolutes and a warped sense of God's purpose for my life made me think that there's always only one "right" decision to every situation I face. This is a severely crippling belief. It not only creates undue pressure as I face countless decisions daily, it can build up to a lifetime of guilt over decisions or actions I think I got wrong.

And as a Christian, if I choose the wrong decision, what if it has eternal consequences? What if my one wrong choice jettisoned me from the holy trajectory I was on, and now I'm hurtling farther and farther away from God's will with each new step? What if I've forfeited God's "best" purpose for me- and forget His "plan B" for my life- I'm left with "plan Z".

Every day there's a "should" dialogue in my head: *Should I call this friend today? Do I need to spend time with my kids right now, or carve out time for me? Should I say yes to this ministry opportunity or say no so that I can serve somewhere else? Am I doing this because I want to or God wants me to? Should we adopt another kid or not? Should I stay at this church, or go to one in the city? Should I text this person to tell them I miss them or will that send them into a shame spiral for not coming around more often? Should I give money to this person, or that cause? Should I fast from peanut butter, or not fast at all? Should I watch TV or ought I to be doing something more spiritual? Should I pick up the hitchhiker, or will that endanger my kids?*

You get it. I live with the mentality that if more than one option exists, there must be a "right" option and I'm obligated to find it without the benefit of omniscience or psychic powers. Too bad I can't use my GPS, because "should" is a tough road to travel.

I wonder if "should" is a twisted piece of the fall that we don't acknowledge much. Adam and Eve were living in the garden walking with God daily. They lived in a strange world, where there was no discerning right from wrong, there was apparently no concept of shame or guilt, just a relationship with God that was as natural as one with flesh and blood. When they ate that fateful fruit, they became aware of right and wrong, but not in the Holy way God sees right from wrong. Instead of helping us live to our fullest, knowledge of right and wrong actually caused us to be somehow drawn to darkness and selfishness.

But beyond that, our humanity took knowledge of "good" too far. Look at the rule-following that we, along with the Pharisees and legalistic Christianity, believed would make us right, make us holy. Perhaps the guilt of my childhood upbringing is really an outcropping of only humanly understanding right from wrong, of no longer trusting that I can find my sense of rightness in a daily walk with God as Adam and Eve did. Instead, my finite understanding of holiness leaves me chasing a false perfection in the form of "should".

One of the most pivotal "should" decisions of my life also served as a catalyst of change in my perception of God's will for my life. I graduated high school in 2005 and spent the next couple years at a community college. Just shy of a two-year degree, I decided to transfer to a Christian college in Pennsylvania about five hours away from home and Jeff, my then boyfriend of a year and a half.

I drastically underestimated how difficult the transfer experience would be. I didn't associate with any particular class so socially I just felt outside and lost. Academically I was no better: I (maybe?) wanted to major in Spanish, but was behind in classes, and for the life of me I couldn't decide what career my Spanish would translate to. Although there were some significant moments of independence and growth for me away at college, I felt like I was paying an awful lot of money to be lonely and ambivalent about career possibilities.

Back home over Christmas break I enjoyed being with my family and friends, and reconnecting with Jeff. I remember sitting with him in a small group from church talking with others about my dilemma. I told one friend that I really didn't want to go back to college, that I just wanted to come home. He said, very matter-of-factly, "Then come home."

My heart argued back: *Um, Maybe you haven't heard, but people don't start college and then drop out. Not good, Christian, responsible people anyway. I mean, the sweet people at my last job sent me off with farewell college gifts and well wishes for moving on to change the world. They think I'm actually doing something with my life. My own father, who had tried to carefully warn me in the first place about heading into too much college debt, supported me anyway by buying me a mini fridge and microwave for my dorm. What would he think?*

I went to college because I felt I *should* go to college, and now I didn't think I could leave because my stubborn sense of "should" said I couldn't.

But my friend's casual comment seemed to weaken my "should"- to somehow give me permission to change course- so I began to seriously consider it. The more I allowed myself to really contemplate returning home, the lighter my heart felt. In a follow up conversation with my dad, I poured out my fears that God had this one path for me to take and that I might be screwing it up if I came home. My dad gave me such an encouraging assurance that God's purpose for our lives isn't always as rigid as we think.

Many times we aren't faced with "right" or "wrong" choices, or even "good" or "better" choices- we simply have more than one choice. We talked about how God doesn't always have a specific "yes" or "no" for our path- He wants us to acknowledge Him, but He may give freedom to choose in certain areas.

And even when we ignore a nudge God may be giving us about a particular direction, He isn't in the business of sending us off to float in a life raft on the sea of poor choices. Our decisions do have consequences, but God is still sovereign- He knew where we might fall, and He very much STILL has a plan for our lives.

So I quit college. (It's still a little crazy to write that out.) Within a year of being home, I got a short term job as a nanny and got married. Then we started having kids, a dream of mine, so I've never gone back to school. I still wonder occasionally what my life would have been like if I'd stayed the college course. I know that God would have used that experience in my life in many amazing ways.

But as my husband reminds me when I lie awake at night trying to figure out my life, the choices I made brought me to where I am today and for all the what ifs, it's a beautiful life. I know God is using me and my family right where we are now, regardless of whether I missed His heart somewhere along the way. In fact, if I'm too focused on knowing God's exact plan for me, might I be losing sight of simply enjoying God's presence? As others have suggested, might I be missing out on the fullness of the present for worrying about the past and future?

So here's to dropping "should" off at the curb and learning to walk with God daily, mistakes and all.

ADOPTION

I don't remember when I first knew I wanted to adopt, but I could argue that a stomach bug is ultimately what forced me to act on that desire. After my first child and my diagnosis of diabetes, I initially felt confident about getting pregnant a second time. With a little surprise, we found out we were expecting again when my daughter was only nine months old. For some reason, the diabetes was harder to manage this time around and with my glucose levels all over the place, my OB asked me if I wanted to have my tubes tied after delivery. I was only 23- did I want my tubes tied? Absolutely not! Even with adoption on the table, I wasn't ready to close that biological door.

But five months into pregnancy, that stomach bug changed my plan. Between my unborn son taking nutrients and my inability to keep anything down, I couldn't maintain my blood sugar levels. I ended up in the ER to get glucose via IV, and later they moved me to the maternity ward of the hospital to monitor the baby through the trauma. Everything turned out fine, but after that moment I decided maybe I didn't want to get pregnant again. It was so stressful knowing my condition was affecting my baby, and feeling so out of control. So I told my doctor I'd changed my mind and immediately after the birth of my sweet boy, I had a tubal ligation.

There's a picture of me with my son, not even a month old, and if you look closely in the background you can see an *Adoption for Dummies* book. You might think that's crazy, but once we'd closed the door to more biological children, I wanted to get my foot in the door for adoption right away. Over the next two years I casually researched both international and domestic adoptions, as our family shifted and moved into a new home.

But in November of 2012, when my kids were two and three years, my husband and I finally started pursuing adoption in earnest. I lived and breathed adoption research- we applied to and had a phone interview with a private adoption agency in CA, before opting instead to look at two local CT agencies. The representative from the first agency made me feel like we'd never be able to afford private adoption, and she seemed very negative towards adopting through the state.

However, our second agency, Connecticut Adoption Services (CAS),[1] had a fantastic representative who listened to us well. Their representative said that, while we could certainly find a way to afford private adoption, she felt that we would be excellent candidates for adopting through the state which, in many cases, has little cost at all.

So in early January, after a month of prayerful consideration, we started an adoption process with CAS. We began taking the mandatory classes for state adoption, started a home study process, and filled out an embarrassing amount of paperwork about ourselves. (If you really want my autobiography, read my adoption application.) As long as we had something to check off our adoption to-do list, I felt like I was in control, as though I could will a baby into our lives.

Just five months later, in June, we were officially licensed! And then came the hard part...passive waiting. People say we're great for taking in a child but the truth is, though I had two precious children, I was deeply longing for another. I prayed for a baby like I've never prayed for anything, but the reality that I could no longer control any part of the process hit me hard.

I don't know why I fight for control so much, when the end of my control is so often where I encounter the living God.

We began getting phone calls about potential children within a week of being licensed, but each call was followed by a bit of heartbreak. We might be an appropriate match for a child, but the state had to sort through perhaps dozens of other available families to see which would be the best placement for each situation. Months went by and I lived for emails from our social worker, my heart always jumping a bit when the phone rang. The more children we said "yes" to that didn't end up being placed with us, the more discouraged I became.

Almost every night when we prayed with the kids I'd pray for a baby. At one point my daughter, then four, said, "Why do we keep praying for a baby? Why is it taking so long?" And while I was glad she could see that prayer isn't the same as a magic-8 ball, I, too, was wondering why God seemed to not be answering. Why would he place the desire on my heart to adopt if He wasn't going to give us a child? I was in a very weird place during this time, seeking God but a little depressed and unsure of how this faith thing was supposed to work.

We waited what seemed a terribly long eight months. Then we got an email about a newborn boy, still in the hospital. We said we'd be willing to take him, but by that time I had difficulty believing we would be chosen. It was a Friday, so we waited out the weekend, trying in vain not to think about the boy until Monday when we knew they would make a decision. Then came the call I had been living for- we had been picked for this baby, who didn't even have a name yet.

Oh and, by the way, could we be at the hospital to take him home in two hours?

My emotions were crazy as I called my husband, crying, to tell him the news- as I told our kids they were getting a baby brother- as we rushed out to meet a little baby we'd no logical claim to, and take him home by some miracle. Then came paperwork, visits with social workers, and the general craziness of life with three young kids. I laughed when people said, "You look great for having just had a baby!", and got teary when I had to fill check off "guardian" instead of "parent" at the pediatrician's office.

But despite all the ups and downs, today that little boy that I prayed for, that I believe God drew us to, is officially adopted into our family.

Looking at my sweet son I find it so incredibly natural that he's part of our family that I forget the years of prayer and baby steps of faith that ultimately brought us to him. My faith has grown through learning to follow the passion God gave us, and watching God do beyond what we could have imagined or orchestrated on our own. In approaching Jesus over and over again to ask for this baby, I began to find more of Jesus himself. I learned to be more raw with God, to be vulnerable and needy and ultimately to chisel away more of the polite but plastic relationship I've sometimes maintained with Him.

The journey didn't look like I planned, but it did lead to an answered prayer- an answer which makes me want to believe God for more, for the next thing He puts on my path that takes me beyond myself. Because faith becomes stale- obsolete even- if we don't act on it. This isn't just a tragedy for others wondering what we stand for, but for ourselves who can live so safely that we are never entirely sure that we need God.

So what's the next thing that's on my heart that I can't possibly do on my own? Is there some crazy passion that burns inside you? If we never act on those God-given pieces of ourselves, how will we truly know if God is big enough to do the impossible- to live up to His promises?

GOD OF THE DETAILS

Do you ever wonder if God really cares about us? I have. Maybe He has time for the BIG life things like marriage and moving across country, but does He care about my day to day? Then I read verses about how God doesn't forget even the sparrow, so he couldn't possibly forget about us who are worth more to him than many sparrows.[2] God says the very hairs on our heads are numbered and known by Him, and that He knows our ways intimately, saw how we were formed, knew us before we existed.[3]

It's a hard concept to grasp and believe: hard to see ourselves as creation, and perhaps harder to see God as a creator who knows and cares deeply about the details of our lives. Because when there's chaos around me, when there's struggle and I call out to God with no apparent answer, it can feel like He doesn't even care to know if I'm alive or not.

Then something seemingly random will happen to me and make me think that God is much more involved in the details of my life than I always see. Maybe we don't recognize God showing up in our details until we learn to trust Him with the details.

One day I packed up all the kids in the car to the go to the grocery store, which is no small feat in itself. We went to Aldi, because it's friendly on our budget, and right after I parked I remembered the obnoxious Aldi cart system. For those that don't know, to get a cart at Aldi you have to bring a quarter to unlock it from the other carts at the cart return area. You get your quarter back when you return your cart, and somehow that's incentive enough to keep people returning their own carts so Aldi doesn't have to pay someone to do it.

Anyway, I forgot to bring a quarter. Nothing in my wallet. I searched the car coin slots; I searched the little compartment in the side door where I usually stuff used tissues. Nothing. I didn't even have enough cash or other coins on me to ask an attendant to exchange money for a quarter. But there was no way I was driving all the way home for a stupid quarter.

It was a pretty exasperating moment.

So I prayed this half-hearted prayer- really not the finest prayer from my repertoire. It had no flowery language, no element of gratitude, no recognition of His holiness. It was more like, "God, I'm pretty frustrated and I don't have a quarter. Could you please just...help me." That was it.

Then I opened the car door and stepped out like a buffoon with no real game plan, and this lady instantly walked over to me. I hadn't even seen her before that very second. She wasn't just any lady- she was the essence of sweet southern motherliness. And she said to me, "Honey, it looks like you could use a cart." I was taken aback, and stammered something about not being able to give her a quarter and she just waved me off and said not to even worry about it. Then she was gone and I was standing there with a cart and there was something in me that knew this wasn't just a coincidence.

Oh, you can call it that- and you can say "why doesn't God always give out free carts?" or "If God can give you a cart, why can't he give food to so and so?" I don't have answers for all that, but I don't have to have all the answers to experience God.

I believe God gives me those moments that almost seem trivial at times to remind me that He *does* see, He *is* watching, He *enjoys* giving when I'm at the very end of my ability. Maybe those are the few times I allow myself to lean on Him. And I write down these moments in my journal so I won't forget where God has met me, just like the Israelites remembered, over and over how God brought them out of Egypt.

Maybe next week I'm back to doubting, but there will always be that voice in the back of my head that says, *"The world is broken-yes- in this world there will be trouble. But don't forget... don't forget what God has done for you. Don't forget about the grocery cart. Don't forget that He cares about this moment right now."*

I'VE GOT SPIRIT

Shortly after Jesus was raised from the dead and returned to Heaven, which was pretty out-there to begin with, there was an almost absurd scene where some of Jesus's disciples first received the Holy Spirit. Acts 2:2 actually says that people "saw what seemed to be tongues of fire that separated and came to rest on each of them."

Um, OK.

So at this point people begin talking about Jesus in other languages so everyone present can understand. And if that isn't strange enough, there are numerous instances in the Old and New Testaments when people heal or speak in the Spirit, or act because they are filled with the Spirit. One guy even gets whisked from one location to another after sharing the gospel with a stranger.[4]

Growing up we learned about the Trinity- how God is three persons in one: Father, Son (Jesus), and Holy Spirit. The whole thing is a mystery to begin with, but the most mysterious piece of the Trinity seemed to be the Spirit. Somehow I think that because it was the hardest to explain, the Spirit was the least talked about. We might say that someone "felt lead" to do something, and maybe an occasional missionary or book would talk about how God did the unexplainable healing, etc. But I never really thought much of what it meant to experience the Spirit.

We even kind of minimized the Spirit in our terminology; we would refer to the act of becoming a Christian as "asking Jesus to come into your heart", as though my heart had a little door and mini Jesus would just kind of take up residence there like a genie. Maybe set up a futon couch or something. With Christ in my heart and God apparently in heaven, where on earth did the Spirit fit in?

I didn't have many people around me exploring the idea of the Spirit till I was a teen. At that time, my mom met weekly with a bunch of women to study through the book of Acts, which talks a lot about the Holy Spirit. Suddenly, several from the group began to "pray in tongues" which they said was a Spirit prayer language but sounded a bit strange to me. It was like my mom and the others were on this journey where they were practicing, if you will- testing what the Bible says about the Spirit to see if there was more that they'd been missing. If it happened in the Bible, why not now? What could it possibly mean that we have the Spirit of God within us?

But I wasn't interested- in fact, I was nervous for my mom. From the outside, the group seemed like a bunch of women getting together and trying to find God in emotions and questionable theology. I'm typically a facts-before-experience person, and this didn't make sense.

Years later, my mom is still convinced there's more to the Holy Spirit than she grew up learning about. She believes her faith in God has been enriched through her journey, but she also found more of her own questions. For myself, though I default to skepticism, I was gradually changed watching my mom let go of preconceived ideas and try to embrace what it means to have the Spirit of God always available to us. I'm on my own journey to understand more of what it means to daily "keep in step with the Spirit".[5]

There are still concepts of the Spirit I struggle with, like healing or prophesying (speaking a word from God), which once sounded a bit far-fetched and outdated to me. It sounded like precarious territory. Maybe Jesus and the disciples healed people back then- maybe there were prophets in the Old Testament, but is that stuff really still happening? Yet I've seen the Spirit work in some unexplainable ways. I still don't know exactly what it means to "pray in the Spirit". Some have said it's a beautiful experience, but others ask "Why do I need a prayer language? Can't God hear my prayers anyway?"

So where does that leave me? I'm certain I've dismissed the Spirit too much growing up, but I'm not certain how to embrace Him now. Ultimately, I've come to see the Spirit as more than just a "Jiminy Cricket" who acts as my conscious: He's the very piece of God that lives in me. Jesus said that He would send His Spirit as an advocate to help and be with us and to teach and remind us what Jesus said.[6] The Bible says that the Spirit gives different gifts in the form of abilities or roles that He creates each of us for.[7]

I believe that the Spirit changes us and gives us qualities like love, joy, peace, patience, kindness, gentleness, and self-control.[8] I'm learning to see how the Spirit really can give us words to say or boldness to speak where we are humanly at a loss. Yet there's still an air of mystery to the Spirit and what His role in our life is supposed to look like. And I think that's exactly as it should be really. Can we ever fully dissect or understand the mystery of God dwelling in us?

Questions surrounding the Spirit shouldn't be surprising, then, but expected. Why does God heal sometimes but not others despite our strong faith? What does it look like to be filled with the Spirit and speak things from God's heart? How do we do that without bringing our humanness into the message- without distorting God's truth from time to time? Why does God sometimes seem to work through the Spirit in more obvious, miraculous ways, and other times we can't see His work until we are looking back at it over months or even decades?

In my attempt to understand more of the Spirit I feel like I'm experimenting with God, which in some ways sounds like a terrible idea. What if my experimenting takes me a little too far down a path that isn't God's real design- that places a bit too much emphasis on my experience of God and not enough emphasis on Him alone? What if I make a huge mistake, and it affects other people?

Where I'm coming to lately is that to pursue God recklessly and take Him at His word is going to take me out of my comfort zone. My faith today has been built on seeing God work and acting on faith in what I've known. Each time I believe Him and see Him at work, I learn something new about Him and I trust Him in a new way. Without trying out God's word for myself, I will never see what God can really do. Without expecting to interact with God, I'll never know Him very well.

At a practical level this means that I'm trying to make space to listen to the Spirit more often. For instance, if I'm reading the Bible, sometimes I will simply ask God to show me what He wants me to read, which at times leads to nothing and that's OK. But other times I've read something that was very much what I needed to hear in that moment and I know it was a God thought. Or sometimes I'll have a dream and wake up and think, *"well God uses dreams to speak to people sometimes"* so I'll pray about whether it means something.

It takes practice to stop listening to the voices of other people in my head, and to stop wondering if I'm hearing God's voice or my own. Sometimes that still small voice just gets drowned out or appears completely silent, but I know the Spirit is still there guiding me. Do I take my trial and error too far sometimes? Of course. Just ask my husband, and he'll have a good chuckle.

But at the end of the day, I don't regret trying to find more of God, whatever that looks like. I don't regret trying to make space to hear and see the miraculous in the everyday things. I may never fully grasp the magnitude of the Spirit of the living God in me, but I don't want to go my whole life without trying to live in that reality.

EXPERIMENT #7:

Perhaps you've never talked to God and expected Him to interact with you. No matter where you are in your walk, I challenge you to try spending time with God in a new way this week. We will all experience God in different ways and atmospheres based on our personality, so begin to notice the things and places that you love, because those are the areas where you may be most likely to connect with God. Even if this feels strange, try at least one of the following this week:

- Try to be more interactive with God during your Bible reading. Before you begin reading, take some time to pray that God will show you a passage or verse. You might want to keep a phone or computer near so you can look up verses if a word or phrase pops into your mind: biblegateway.com is a fantastic online resource that lets you search for key words/topics in whatever Bible version you prefer to use. Even if you don't feel that God is impressing you with anything specific (which is OK!), ask Him to speak to you personally as you read any passage in the Bible. If you need a place to start, you might try one of the four gospels (Matthew, Mark, Luke or John) which tell about the life of Jesus. If anything sticks out to you, write it down or pray about it.

- Sometimes being aware that God is interacting with us personally simply begins with expecting Him to. Act on a nudge to give to someone, call someone, go somewhere, or do something God might be directing you to do, even if it feels silly. Don't overthink. You may even find that God works through something that felt like a "coincidence" because God is always at work behind the scenes. Write about what happened when you took your baby step of faith this week.

- Spend several minutes listening to worship music or sitting outside alone, etc. (You can use online worship from Pandora or make a playlist on Spotify if you don't own worship music.) Focus more on listening to God and being with Him and His presence than in talking to Him. Maybe try kneeling, lifting your hands, or even dancing if you feel like it. Experimenting with our posture and the different ways we can worship helps us to step outside of a plastic relationship and routine. It might feel strange and that's OK. Reflect on how God meets you, speaks to you, or leads you to worship.

- Do something that you love- playing music, going for a walk, working out at the gym, painting or creating through art, writing, dancing, hiking, _____ (insert your own). As you do, consider that God is with you in this activity, and that He enjoys this about you because He made you to enjoy it. Reflect on how it feels to know that you can meet God anywhere- even in things that don't feel "spiritual".

8
GRAY ANSWERS

JESUS THE SQUIRREL

There's an old joke about a little boy in Sunday school: The teacher asks the class, "What is gray, has a bushy tail, and eats nuts?" The boy responds, "Well, I know the answer must be Jesus, but it sure sounds like a squirrel to me."

Growing up in church meant going to Sunday school classes. We learned Bible stories about Adam and Eve, Jonah and the whale (which we stopped saying once we found out it was technically a "big fish"), Moses and, of course, Jesus. My mom taught Sunday school often, and she'd use a "flannel graph" board which is pretty much what it sounds like- a big board with a flannel fabric on it and small felt Bible characters to represent the story we were learning. Hey, it was the days before iPads and we were low budget anyway, but it worked pretty well. Except that the characters always had to awkwardly face in one direction because they were blank on the back. Jesus might tell Peter to "follow me" and Peter could, but he would have to follow backwards.

As a child the Bible seemed to offer such simple answers for everything. Are you feeling afraid? "When I am afraid, I put my trust in you".[1] Do you want to accomplish something? "I can do all things through Christ who strengthens me".[2] How do we know God loves us? "He gave his one and only Son".[3]

As a child I felt that there must be a "right" or at least a spiritual answer for everything. I took pride in having the answers because I had the Bible, which was supposed to make everything make sense. As the song goes, *"Jesus loves me—this I know/ For the Bible tells me so;"*. [4]

There's this thought that the Bible says it, I believe it, end of story.

But even though the Bible gives wisdom and guidance for living, it's full of things that are confusing, hard to agree on, and sometimes downright shocking. I believe God inspired the Bible and that Jesus is the Word of life for us. But that doesn't mean I don't struggle with the Bible. That doesn't mean I can't question the Bible when I don't understand, nor does it mean I have to throw the Bible out the window when I'm confused by it.

Understanding the Bible as God's message to us is a beautiful thing. I believe it can change lives. Period. But those of us who you grew up in the church have a knack for glossing over the parts of the Bible that are sticky or messy or too controversial. Especially with kids. Even now as I help teach children's classes at church, I'm struck by how we often reduce the Bible stories to a simple, positive takeaway. (Bonus points if we can turn into a memorizable axiom and shout it as a group.)

At some level I know that we have to simplify stories for kids, that we'll traumatize them if we tell them all the gritty details of every Bible story. Perhaps five year olds don't need to know that the prophets of Baal ran around slashing themselves bloody while trying to get their god to listen to them,[5] or that our hero Noah was found drunk and naked in his tent.[6] But we also sometimes gloss over the gray places of Christianity; we often favor the simple answers to the complex ones- or to no answer at all.

But I wonder what message this sends to our kids. Do we set our youth up to be disillusioned when they grow older and first encounter something in the world that their faith doesn't seem to answer? Do we set the stage at this early age for the prevalent mindset in church that doubts and struggles shouldn't be shared because they might mean something is wrong with us? I wonder at what age we have to get beyond just telling kids the nuts and bolts of faith and let them experience the raw stories- the real questions. I wonder how often we're honest with our kids about the limitations of our knowledge.

My daughter is six and she's been asking some hard questions for years. Once as I was explaining how God made the world from nothing, she spat out, "How did God get here?" I told her it was a good question, and I didn't have a good answer. I awkwardly rambled on about it a bit, but I ended by saying, "It's kind of confusing isn't it?" I could pretend up an answer- I could tell her that God is God and that's all the answer she needs. But that wouldn't be fair. I've had to wrestle myself through the idea that my faith in God might answer how I exist, but not how He does. I will have to let her wrestle through that too.

Honestly, when I try to explain my faith to my children I sometimes feel so impossibly plastic. I so want them to tangibly feel the presence of God the way I have- to know Him- to see that this faith offers both practical wisdom and sustenance for the soul. But sometimes the words come out so stiff; sometimes in my attempt to make it all make sense I over-simplify.

I don't think we're meant to have all the answers here and now. 1 Corinthians 13:12 says, "For now we see only a reflection as in a mirror; then we shall see face to face. Now I know in part; then I shall know fully, even as I am fully known." No matter how much we study the Bible, no matter how much revelation we may get, or how much we come to know God through the years, we will always only know in part here on earth. We aren't going to see all the behind the scenes events. We won't see fully into the future for all our prayers, and we can't satisfactorily prove the origins of earth no matter how hard we dig.

There is going to be mystery. We don't have all the answers.

We also have to learn and teach our kids that even "right" answers aren't always helpful. We live in a physical world with physical needs and problems. Yes there are spiritual answers and solutions to things, but sometimes we try too hard to use those as a quick fix to problems. When someone loses a loved one, when we see hurt and suffering or encounter struggle, we want to make it better. If we could just explain the pain in a way that makes sense, maybe we could give it purpose and take away the sting.

We go on the defensive other times and want to prove "God is still good! You can still believe! He will fix this, you'll see!" Sometimes we have to be comfortable being uncomfortable. We have to understand that even the best Biblical answer isn't a quick fix; it doesn't remove all doubt, and doesn't need to. Sometimes the most spiritual answer is the "squirrel" answer, and sometimes it's OK to not answer at all.

FORMULAS SCHMORMULAS

If you go online right now you could easily find a plethora of quizzes to take about yourself: "What animal matches your personality?", "Are you an extrovert or introvert?", "Which 'Friends' character you would be?" I don't think we can help ourselves; we're drawn to the idea of inputting our preferences and personality traits into some system which spits out the results to who we are.

The Christian world has its quizzes too, from personality types to "which spiritual gift do you have?" Yes. There's a quiz somewhere of things you enjoy doing, which correlate to a spiritual gift. You're supposed to put a number from one to five to indicate your interest in each of the activities, tally up your points in a corresponding spiritual gifts grid and, voila! You should have discovered your spiritual gift. Or your top two. Or in my case, since I answered with a lot of threes, your top ten.

As much as I get sucked into those tests, I think I end up hating them every time. They can give me an idea about myself, but there's no point system quiz on the planet that can wrap up the complexity of who I am into a box, label me, and tell me that I'm in the same group as a million other people. As soon as I'm labeled, I tend to get a bit uncomfortable and claustrophobic. I get the itch to tear my label off and make a new one, but I'm a bit wordy so it would come out as a paragraph and no one would take it seriously.

The part of me that likes quizzes wants to be easily defined so I can easily define the path I should take in life. But deep down I know that life isn't that simple.

Just as our squirrel answers and personal quizzes oversimplify, sometimes we try to boil down all the problems of life to simple formulas that should work for everyone. *"Do you have trouble in your marriage? Fix it with these three easy steps." "Do you want to know how to raise the perfect kids? Here's ten things to try!" "You, too, can get closer to God through our twenty day program! Guaranteed!"*

Here's a shocker- I'm not a formula person. Maybe you are. But a formula is only good as long as it's working. And if it doesn't work, is it broken or are you? Formulas pretend that what works for a few people will work for all people. Formulas make life sound like it can always be fixed if we put enough effort in. Formulas can guide, but they don't truly have any power over our problems.

I'd say "formulas don't fix problems, God does!" but I can't tell you how or when. We aren't math equations to be solved with the right algorithms; we're human beings, and God works in each of us in such a personal way if we are open to Him.

Faith isn't formulaic. Faith is an organic thing, germinating in the soil of our unique experience with God. I'm so thankful to be surrounded by people who hold firmly to their faith, who guide me through their own experience, and encourage me on my journey. But please do not tell me that your story will be mine. I pray I don't pretend my story should be yours. I deeply cherish my faith, but there isn't a formulaic magic that gave it to me, nor is there a formula with which to pass it to my kids. I don't have faith because of perfect answers and solutions. I have faith because of perfect Love that meets me where I am.

I THINK THEREFORE I AM

At the risk of being painfully redundant, I'd like state that I have fewer solid answers now than ever. I'm love to underline and write notes in my Bible, and there are many places where I simply put a question mark. Some things I flat out don't understand (see most of Revelation for starters). Then there are other places where God seems uncomfortably harsh, or Paul says something that sounds a little misogynistic, or one verse seems to contradict another part of the Bible. So I have no problem putting a question mark and digging deeper into the meaning.

I also surround myself with friends who have no choice but to humor my need for theological conversations, although these often just produce more questions. See, I live with the not-so-tiny problem of having a faith that I can't always prove. I have experiences of faith that continue to confirm what I believe, but so often that seems a pretty flimsy answer for those who haven't been on the same journey.

So if I struggle with parts of the Bible- if I can't prove all aspects of my faith- why do I believe any of it?

For me that starts with deconstructing what I believe. Just as Descartes used "I think therefore I am" as a fundamental premise for knowledge, I have a couple of foundational beliefs apart from the Bible even that ground me in my faith.

My first principle is simply that I believe truth exists. So many people say that we should "live and let live"- that I can believe what I believe and you believe what you believe and it will all work out for both of us. In fact, we tend to think that anyone who can't accept religious pluralism is a closed-minded bigot. One definition of religious pluralism is the "acceptance of the concept that two or more religions with mutually exclusive truth claims are equally valid".[7]

Religions with mutually exclusive truths may all be "valid" but if they are all "truth" then really none of them are truth. As much as I believe that everyone has a right to believe whatever they want, I also believe that truth cannot be relative. In other words, we can't believe one thing without disbelieving something else. If I'm searching for truth, at some point I'm going to bump into something that isn't.

I realize this doesn't prove that Christianity itself is true, but it's a very basic reason for me to put so much faith in faith.

My second driving principle for faith is the existence of a complex universe and people. In moments of uncertainty I've tried to suspend my belief in God to see where that would leave me. Would it be freeing? Would it make more sense? But time after time I get stuck when I look at the sky, when I think about the intricacy of people and even the complexity of science. At the end of the day I can't come to grips with the idea that we're here without intentional design.

I realize many don't see the world as evidence of God, but try as I might, I can't seem to understand life any other way. Has the natural process of adaptation helped form the world as we know it? I would say yes. Can I prove that God created the world? No. Do I think that it requires faith for me to believe in a creator I can't see? Yes. But to be honest, one also must have faith to believe in a world where matter exists without a creator.

If it's so simple, why doesn't everyone believe as I do? Exactly. One of the very tensions I must wrestle with is that my most foundational premises of faith are not universal. Your most basic experience may have lead you to the exact opposite conclusion. However, if truth exists, then even the parts of life that I can't explain are based in a truth. So this faith is really my journey to experience truth- to explore truth- to put truth to the test.

I hope that means that my faith journey will always leave me seeking truth, even if I have to find it in the gray things of life. And if you've never stopped to think about the fundamental reasons that make your beliefs tick, it's a worthwhile exercise.

THE SUFFERING DILEMMA

"I want to believe in God, but how does God fit in with a suffering world? If He is so good, why do horrible things happen?" These are typical questions that hold people back from faith, and they call my own belief into question at times. In chapter six I wrestled through my own piece of this broken world, but how can I make sense of the drastically worse suffering of others- of starvation, child abuse and trafficking, cancer and heartache?

My best answers often feel like a dismissal of the tragedy. They can't seem to reach into the depths of the grief and brokenness that plague this world. So I echo, why doesn't God intervene? Why does He allow wickedness to persist?

Even if people don't believe in God or an afterlife, I think there's we agree that this life is not what it should be- that something is very wrong and needs to be fixed. I believe that the world was once beautiful and harmonious in Eden, and that it will be again one day. But that still leaves the slight issue of the in between- the now. Why do we have to wait on perfection?

At one level, I think we underestimate the two-sided gift of choice that makes us human. I suppose we could come into this world pre-programmed with an internal mechanism that stops us from taking any action that will harm us or others. The world would certainly be a simpler place. But a program that would keep us from making "wrong" choices would also make our love and joy and our thoughts not really our own.

To remove the choice from our love, from our lives, is to remove the lifeblood from our being and the significance from our actions. All that would be left behind is robotic emotion, thoughts devoid of authenticity and substance. We couldn't produce real love for each other or for God- all of that would be automatic. What kind of world would that look like? Would it be better? Is it possible that the meaning of our lives would be lost without choice?

But there's risk inherent in choice. Choice may make us genuine but it opens us up to brokenness, which is exactly the story of Adam and Eve. They chose not to trust God, and every successive choice, right or wrong, is affected by that first one. Now, not only do each of us make choices that hurt other people, we also must react to other people's wrong choices. The world spirals onward and even if most of our decisions seem good, humanity as a whole seems to be drifting farther away from perfection.

I've wondered what would happen if God started taking away that freedom of choice, just the really bad things at first. Maybe He'd start with the evil of murder, of child-abuse, the unthinkables. But where would we draw the line? He'd have to stop each of us eventually, because it seems even the worst actions stem from this little problem of selfishness and that's what makes us all go wrong.

Or perhaps God could just hit a reset button and remove the current "evil". But, as my husband once said, if God left us with our choices and simply fixed all that was wrong with the world right now, how long would it take for us to mar Eden again?

I also have to wonder what it means to us that this world is full of so many things that can be described only as evil. The presence of evil invites a whole debate of its own. Does evil imply a constant law of basic morality, and if so, who gets to decide what constitutes "good"? Who gets to decide what is "evil"? If there IS a higher power or force of good, I'm left to question why bad things still happen, or even blame bad things on God.

But if there's NOT a higher power or force of good, what then? Is there any chance we can even agree on what's best for the world, let alone implement change that can reverse the damage? As my dad put to me once, if everyone can choose their own morality, do we even get to say that someone else is "wrong", regardless of whether they lie on their taxes or abuse a child? What possible hope are we living for if there's no one great enough to even label the worst of this world as wrong?

And then there's heaven, which may sometimes ring of a fairy tale (an image not helped by depictions of cherubs with tiny harps bouncing on clouds). But what if heaven is really the promise of a new creation- a doing away with the curse and brokenness of this world? What if heaven is God's ultimate answer of justice- to set things right again? Heaven becomes the new earth where God reigns over all who chose to love Him.

I can't explain all evil, but I accept it because I believe God is ultimately going to act. The evil of the world already stands condemned and justice is coming, albeit in God's timing.[8]

But heaven would be a pretty pitiful remedy if it were just for later, when we die. Jesus brought heaven to earth so that heaven exists anywhere that God is allowed to reign here and now. When we surrender ourselves to God we will inevitably find the places where heaven meets earth. Often through the mystery of prayer we find God to be active, working against evil here and now, starting by renewing our own hearts and minds. Only when we engage heaven here do we find that we can truly confront evil.[9]

The beauty of this world and the suffering alike tell me that we were meant for more- they make me long for a world to come. But just because I believe in the world to come, I don't wrestle less with the pain of humanity now. Nor do I think that God's ultimate justice gives me a reason to sit back and watch the world suffer if I can do something about it. I believe the very things we sow here in earth through God will be part of what's eternal. Our actions very much matter; in fact our love and faith without action is dead and worthless.[10]

So it turns out I don't have the perfect answer for suffering- maybe not even a satisfying answer. But I find enough evidence of love and hope in the world that I'm learning to accept suffering even when I don't fully understand.

FAITH EXISTS IN THE TENSION

I recently heard Pete Wilson (pastor of Cross Point Church in Nashville, TN) speak at a "Women of Faith" conference. For those that know me, a pure estrogen Christian event isn't necessarily my thing. But I volunteered for World Vision[11] so I got in for free, and actually really enjoyed myself. Still, I prefered to bring along a like-minded friend so I could do an eye roll every once in awhile at the cliches of both our gender and our faith.

Anyway, Pete made this comment that we all have belief and unbelief in our heart- that faith is simply choosing to act on belief. And for someone as hyper-analytical, as inside-my-head and full of questions as I am, that was such a freeing statement. God wants my belief and faith, but He's not in the business of only using people who never have a moment of doubt.

Most of our great Bible heroes have bouts with questions. Look at Peter literally walking in faith on top of the water only to sink when he stopped focusing on Jesus.[12] What about John the Baptist who spent his life preparing people for God's kingdom, only to wonder later on if perhaps Jesus wasn't the real deal.[13] Then there's Sarah who doubted God's promise of a son,[14] and Jesus Himself basically asks God if there's another way to save the world, though He alone remained in faith, loving God and the world fully despite the cost.[15]

The Christian faith doesn't preclude questions, doubt, fear or uncertainty.

The more I've learned, the more unanswered questions I've collected. And I wonder at times how I can be so completely sure that I've experienced the living, active God-yet still be so bewildered by my doubts, by my inability to explain everything. But while others may dislike it, or feel unable to stand firm on it, I'm absolutely thriving on the tension of faith-this knowing but not having it all figured out yet.

I can believe in God not because I have all the answers here on Earth now or ever- but because my experience in Him is enough. It's enough to push me to know Him more when at my core I'm wondering why He won't show Himself. It's enough to make me cry out to Him one more time in my moment of need though I can't see His hand yet. It's enough to make me long for more of His presence when I've been away too long. It's enough to sustain my heart and soul when I'm full of grief or fear.

One of the most critical lessons of my life has been to accept this thing of tension: the tension of differences, of ambiguous morality, of answered and unanswered prayer; the tension of sheltering our kids, loving the broken, living in the church; the tension of God's sovereignty and human freedom.

As much as I want happy resolution at the end of my movies, I'm becoming far more confident and content living in the reality that in this life I won't find complete resolution. I'm in process and God is still revealing Himself to me; this world is broken but being redeemed, I'm partly right and partly wrong. And as strange as it may seem to many of you, the tension is one of the things I most want to pass on to my kids.

Because the alternatives to tension are to deny ourselves permission to doubt (plastic faith) or to deny ourselves permission to believe.

LOVE IS MY ANSWER

No one seems to argue much about love. We search out love from our youngest days and flourish under its care. We're drawn to love and we sense that our best moments are driven by it. If I took a quick poll, we'd generally agree: love makes the world a better place. But even love is broken at times.

We love as humans. Sometimes we have the right heart but our love pushes too hard, overprotects, blinds us to what we don't want to see. I love my children deeply but that love on its own can't consistently keep me from lashing out in anger, from over-indulging them, from responding to them in selfishness. Why is love so hard for us when it's the absolute best we can offer each other? Is there perfect love to be found?

I've struggled to find a love that fully fulfills me in this life. Of all the human relationships in my life, none completely fills the deepest soul longing of my heart. Honestly, my relationship with Jesus is a constantly evolving thing, a sometimes frustrating thing, but I'm growing to find that His love really is the one thing I'm most craving. I can't describe to you exactly how or when Jesus began to be more real and present to me. It didn't happen all at once, but bit by bit, in my most vulnerable moments, He showed Himself to be more real than my surroundings.

Something shifted from me praying to Him because He's supposed to be there and I'm supposed to talk to Him. He doesn't want my piety, He wants me to sit and be with Him, just as Mary sat at His feet engaged in His every word.[16] Over time my relationship stopped being so one-way. I've encountered Him in ways that made me think "Oh, hello! You're the God I've been reading about my whole life!"

Did I just believe with my head before and if so when did my heart wake up to Him? How can I believe-my-heart-out but still be surprised by the presence of Jesus? What does it really look like to *know* God?

Beginning to know Jesus means giving up mere belief that he exists, and starting to interact with Him. It's giving Him all that I have and am, and asking Him to show me Himself, His power, His wisdom. I've come to this place where Jesus is truly the sustainer of my being, my constant and precious companion through everything. Even when I don't understand my life or my circumstances, I know this Jesus who eclipses it all, permeates it all, meets me in it all.

I can't imagine life without my Jesus. And not in a "I-can't-imagine-life-without-coffee" kind of way. For a java lover like me that would be a nightmare. But to lose Jesus- well that would be the end of my world. To lose Jesus would be to lose hope, to lose my center of love, to lose my best friend and my very identity.

There's no place that I've been in this life where Jesus wasn't available. I found Him in the long stay at a hospital, sleep-deprived and waiting days to be discharged with my newborn son. I feel Him at the beach, looking out to where the water meets the sky and opening my arms to the warm salt breeze. I marvel at Him when I savor an unexpected laugh with my children, or the look of wonder in their eyes when they experience something new.

His Spirit guides even when I don't feel like following, when every fiber of my being is overwhelmed with this life. Through the empty and the full, the grief and joy, the fear and the peace…He is my constant. I tell God things I don't know how to tell anyone else, and I bring Him the brunt of my burdens and fears and requests. I find comfort in the way He makes the Bible speak to me, and how He gives me His thoughts and direction.

I don't want to pretend that I'm as close to Jesus as I want to be. There are choices I make that distance me from Him, there are countless ways I'm growing to understand Him better. But that's the beauty of any relationship with someone you love, right? You want to pursue them, to know what they're thinking, and study their heart. And you never reach a point where you think you've learned all there is to know about them.

The beautiful thing about a relationship with God is that He made me, so He's already intimately acquainted with who I am. There's nothing I can say that will surprise Him or catch Him off guard.
Unlike all my other relationships, He is perfect. So when I'm angry and lash out or stubbornly refuse to be with Him, He never shuts me out. He never throws my mess back in my face. He never acts selfishly or wishes me harm. That is love; Love that would give all of itself- that would literally die for me- whether I ever chose to accept His sacrifice or not. I can think of no greater love.

I may have doubts- I may have days or even seasons of searching and questioning. Perhaps I have more questions than answers. This faith is messy, gray, and certainly hard. But my hope, my firm anchor and my final answer is simply this incredible, unexplainable Love.

EXPERIMENT #8:

Whatever you believe has been shaped by many things. I challenge you to take away the books, the friend's opinions that fill your head, even the things you were taught to believe as a child. When you strip away all these things, what is the bottom line of your belief- the fundamental reason you believe as you do. Sometimes this means mentally suspending what you believe momentarily to ask yourself if another way makes sense. For example, can you imagine that God doesn't exist? Would your life be substantially changed if He didn't? What, if any, personal experiences have you had with God that shape your belief? Even if you don't feel like you have all the answers, imagine what living out your deepest beliefs may look like in your practical life.

STUDY GUIDE

Welcome to the Gray Faith Study Guide. This is ideal for small groups, as you'll find that different people with unique experiences bring a healthy diversity of answers, as well as new questions! However, the study can easily be done on your own, as a journey to better understand your own story and faith.

There are eight sections, corresponding to each of the eight chapters. In every section you'll find questions meant to help you dig deeper into your personal story and faith experience, and to challenge you to confront the hard questions of Christianity. Many of the questions require some soul-searching, so I recommend that you go over them on your own first even if you are going through the study with a group.

Each study section ends with Bible passages to explore on your own. I'm not perfect and I certainly don't have all the answers. I expect that you won't agree completely with me or even those in your study group! You won't be able to get much out of the study if you aren't willing to allow yourself and others to be completely vulnerable and honest.

But my desire is that in the questions and even disagreements, you learn to seek the answers for yourself in Scripture. As you journey through my stories and questions in the book and study guide, I pray you'll experience the God who is bigger than "good Christianity"; I hope you'll be able to relive your own stories and stand a bit more confident in your own "gray faith".

CHAPTER 1 STUDY QUESTIONS

1. What's your story? Who are the people and circumstances that most shaped your life and faith?

2. In the first section of chapter one, I talk about how "good Christianity" lied to me. Have you experienced your own assumptions of "good Christianity"? If so, what has made you question those assumptions?

3. Read the parable of the Lost Son in Luke 15:11-32. When it comes to experiencing God's grace, which brother do you relate to and why?

4. Who has inspired you to step out in faith or to find more genuine faith?

5. What is your God-given passion beyond your means to produce or create on your own? Whether it's something you're still dreaming about or you're in the middle of living it out, I challenge you to share that dream with someone and let them pray and journey with you.

6. What does it look like to accept brokenness, doubts, and mistakes as part of our journey of faith, or our children's?

7. Are there any beliefs that you hold in your head that you've struggled to experience with your heart? What's one small step you could take to embrace that belief physically, instead of just mentally?

BIBLE PASSAGES FOR FURTHER STUDY

Luke 15:11-32 *(the parable of the prodigal son)*; Deuteronomy 6:1-3 *(passing faith to our kids)*; Proverbs 22:6 *(raising children)*; Galatians 3 *(faith vs. the law)*; Matthew 9:13 *(Jesus came for sinners)*; Luke 18:18-35 *(heart vs. rules)*

CHAPTER 2 STUDY QUESTIONS

1. Do you believe the Christian culture around you has any negatives or unhealthy ideas? Why or why not?

2. We've had our negative moments, but Christian culture often sparks very positive movements. What should "Christian Culture" be doing/influencing and how can we help?

3. "Someone who exposes themselves to a wide variety of ideas might actually be in a healthier place than someone who views outside ideas as dangerous." Agree or disagree? Explain.

4. What is our "Jesus Stuff" (bumper stickers, billboards, shirts, etc.) saying to the world? Discuss how you have experienced/used Christian paraphernalia in a positive or negative way.

5. How does dividing the Bible into "good guys" and "bad guys" keep us from examining our own lives or acknowledging our universal brokenness?

6. Discuss what it looks like to "keep ourselves from being polluted by the world" (James 1:27), while also being the "light of the world" (Matthew 5:14). How can we protect the purity of ourselves and our families while still exposing ourselves to the world that God wants us to love?

7. What words or phrases from your Christian circle might be confusing to someone from outside your group? How do we help bridge the gap in translation?

BIBLE PASSAGES FOR FURTHER STUDY

James 1:27 (*don't be polluted by the world*); Matthew 5:14 (*light of the world*); Romans 12:1-2 (*don't conform to the world*); 1 Thessalonians 5:19-22 (*test everything*); 1 John 4:1-3 *(test every Spirit)*; 1 Corinthians 5:9-13 *(living among sin)*; Matthew 11:19 *(Jesus was friends with sinners)*

CHAPTER 3 STUDY QUESTIONS

1. What is the role or purpose of the local and global church?

2. We want our churches to be relevant and inviting to the outside world for good reason. But have you ever gotten more caught up in what church looked like than the God who is relevant regardless? What does it mean to be "seeker-friendly" in a way that doesn't diminish God?

3. How have you experienced the brokenness of the church? How have you been a part of the brokenness of the church?

4. If you've never done this before, sit down and make a list of church "non-negotiables": the doctrines and practices that you MUST agree with in order to be part of a church family. Then make a list of "secondary issues", such as worship style, ministries or activities offered, etc.

How often do your church frustrations stem from the list of non-negotiables vs secondary issues?

5. All of us within a church family have weaknesses. What does it look like to stay together as a church and balance each other even through disagreements?

6. How can routine and comfort keep us from experiencing God fully in the church?

7. When you consider that some people will never enter a church building, how do you feel? What does it mean for you to be the church outside of the church building?

8. In what areas of ministry do you serve the church? Do you feel that you are serving in a healthy way? (Consider your time commitment, effect on family, energy spent, motivation for serving, people you may feel the need to please, etc.) Have you ever stepped back to reflect and pray about your role?

9. Discuss the cost of our lack of unity between churches, especially across cultural and denominational lines. How can we begin to bridge the gap?

BIBLE PASSAGES FOR FURTHER STUDY

The Book of Acts (*beginning of the Church*); Romans 12:3-13 (*the church as a body*); 1 Corinthians 12:12-31 (*the church as a body*); Hebrews 10:23-25 (*encourage and meet together*); 1 Corinthians 14 (*instructions for worship/ order*)

CHAPTER 4 STUDY QUESTIONS

1. What did you grow up believing were the "big sins"? Has your understanding of or reaction to these sins changed over time?

2. Can you live in the tension that someone else who loves God may not follow God the same way you do? Explain.

3. What is the difference between standing up for what we believe in and arguing with someone over belief?

4. What does it look like to confront sin in love?

5. We're all broken- prone to fail and fall short of God's glory. How have honest relationships in your life have helped to break down your judgment towards others?

6. The "discomfort of grace" means that we all rely on God because we're partly right, partly wrong. Discuss what implications this has for our moral disagreements and how we interact with others.

7. How does reflecting on God's holiness keep us humble before God and others?

BIBLE PASSAGES FOR FURTHER READING

Romans 14 (*don't judge, disputable issues are between us and God*); Matthew 18:15-17 (*sin in the church*); 1 Corinthians 13:9-12 (*we know in part*); Philippian 1:4-11 (*God continues a good work in us*); Luke 7:36-47 (*those who are forgiven much, love much*); Luke 17:1-4 (*causing to sin*); John 8:1-11 (*a woman caught in adultery*); Acts 2:38 (*repent from sin and be forgiven*); Luke 18:9-14 (*humility before God*); 1 Corinthians 5:12-13 (*not judging those outside the church*); Revelation 1:9-18 (*a vision of holy Jesus*)

CHAPTER 5 STUDY QUESTIONS

1. What does it mean to be "saved"?

2. Share what or who has influenced you to start following God, or to continue following Him?

3. Discuss the idea of conversion as a before and after experience. How can we emphasize God's change in our lives without glossing over the reality of our ongoing struggles?

4. Do you feel confident sharing your faith outside of church? Discuss your fears or the reasons for your confidence.

5. How can the pressure to "evangelize" someone undermine the relational aspect of sharing the gospel?

6. A quote attributed to Francis of Assisi says, "Preach the Gospel at all times and when necessary use words." Some use this to suggest our actions should be speaking the gospel louder than our words. Others have said that this quote gives the false impression that using words to share the gospel isn't that important. What does it mean for us to combine the power of our words and actions?

7. My parents once met a man from Africa who was a missionary to America. Does this surprise you? Use this as a springboard to discuss some of the unhealthy views we in America may have regarding mission work. Then discuss some of the positives of missions, perhaps from your own experience.

8. How can examining our view of evangelism and missions help us to love the world better?

BIBLE PASSAGES FOR FURTHER READING

1 Peter 3:15 (*share faith with gentleness and respect*); 1 Peter 2:12 (*how to live among unbelievers*); James 2:15-17 (*action accompanies faith*); Matthew 28:19-20 (*Jesus commands us to share our faith*); Romans 10:11-15 (*why we bring good news*); Acts 2:42-47 (*true godly community attracts others*)

CHAPTER 6 STUDY QUESTIONS

1. What does it look like to give God "an honest acknowledgement of struggle" instead of a "pretense of praise"?

2. What have been some of the "hard places" in your life? Have those places grown your faith or turned you away from God? Why?

3. Discuss how you've experienced God through prayer. Talk about your expectations, disappointments, and your level of honesty with God.

4. What does it look like to give up control and let God author your story? Is this idea scary or liberating for you?

5. Do you believe that God's promises will keep you safe, thriving, and blessed? Use Scripture to explain why or why not.

6. How can we believe in a good God when life doesn't go as we want or expect?

BIBLE PASSAGES FOR FURTHER READING

Psalm 13 (*David honest before God*); Matthew 16:24-25 (*giving up to follow Christ*); Romans 8:28 (*He's working for our good*); John 16:33 (*Jesus promises trouble/He overcomes*); Philippians 4:6-7 (*praying in all situations*); Matthew 5:3-12 (*blessings according to Jesus*); Luke 12:15 (*warning against greed*)

CHAPTER 7 STUDY QUESTIONS

1. How has "should" controlled your life or kept you from enjoying your journey? What would you let go of or do differently today if you weren't so concerned about what you "should" do?

2. A friend once told me that God is like a good parent. As parents we don't expect our kids to ask us about every little decision they make; we enjoy watching them create and make decisions on their own and be themselves. How does our view of God affect our interaction with Him?

3. Share a time when God met you in the details of your life.

4. "I don't know why I fight for control so much, when the end of my control is so often where I encounter the living God." Can you relate to this statement? Explain.

5. Read Psalm 139. How does this passage give you understanding of God's view of you and the details of your life?

6. What does it look like to walk with the Spirit and let Him lead you?

7. Does following God feel routine to you or has it felt like a bit of an experiment? When do you feel most alive in your interactions with God?

8. How can we learn to embrace our possible "mistakes" in our attempts to seek God? Discuss the importance of having godly friends (who don't all think just like we do!) to challenge us along the way and keep us balanced.

BIBLE PASSAGES FOR FURTHER READING

Micah 6:8 (*what God requires of us*); Romans 8:26 (*the Spirit intercedes for us*); Galatians 5:16 (*walk by the Spirit*); John 4:23-24 (*worship in spirit and truth*); Matthew 10:29-31 (*our worth to God*); John 3:5-8 (*life in the Spirit*); 1 Corinthians 10:31 (*do everything for God's glory*); Colossians 3:16-17 (*do everything in the name of Jesus*)

CHAPTER 8 STUDY QUESTIONS

1. What does it mean to be "comfortable being uncomfortable" when we don't have the answers? Why is this necessary?

2. Formulas can be tools to help us grow, but how can they become negative?

3. Imagine/discuss what you believe Eden was like: a perfect relationship with God, a world before the curse. How do you see brokenness of the fall in everything humans have touched?

4. Respond to this statement: "The beauty of the world and the suffering alike tell me that we were meant for more."

5. How or when have you experienced Jesus to be bigger than your circumstances?

6. Be honest with yourself/ your group, and God- what are some the unanswered questions in your life?

7. How can you live with questions and still actively believe in God?

BIBLE PASSAGES FOR FURTHER READING

Romans 1:18-20 (*God reveals Himself through creation*); Mark 9:14-29 (*Jesus heals a boy/father asks for help with unbelief*), Matthew 11.1-6 (*John the Baptist questions Jesus' identity*); Luke 14:28-33 (*wrestle through the cost of following Jesus*); 1 Corinthians 13:8-13 (*knowing in part/ love remains*)

NOTES

Chapter 1: Gray Beginnings

1. Romans 3:10
2. Luke 15:11-32
3. Luke 15:29
4. Luke 15:31
5. 1 Corinthians 4:20
6. Genesis 12:1
7. Matthew 25:40

Chapter 2: Gray Christian Culture

1. Romans 12:2
2. John 3:16
3. Romans 5:8
4. Matthew 12
5. 1 Corinthians 15:19
6. John 4:1-26

Chapter 3: Gray Church

1. Exodus 3:14
2. Hebrews 13:8
3. Luke 9:23
4. Acts 2:42-47
5. Matthew 18:20
6. 2 Corinthians 12:20
7. John 17:22-23
8. Isaiah 56: 6-7

Chapter 4: Gray Sin

1. Exodus 20:7
2. Romans 5:8
3. 1 Corinthians 13:12
4. Isaiah 53:2

5. Revelation 1:8
   6. 1 Peter 1:14-16

Chapter 5: Gray Evangelism

   1. 1 Peter 3:15
   2. James 1:27
   3. Luke 9:23
   4. Matthew 6:11

Chapter 6: Gray Expectations

   1. Matthew 6:9-13
   2. Philippians 4:6
   3. Ecclesiastes 5:2
   4. Romans 8:28
   5. Philippians 4:19
   6. Ezekiel 4
   7. Job 2:9
   8. Job 38:4
   9. Job 38:12
   10. Job 39:27
   11. Job 42: 3
   12. Hebrews 12:2
   13. John 3:16

Chapter 7: Gray Walk

   1. Connecticut Adoption Services, a program of Waterford Country School. 2 Clinic Drive, Norwich, CT 06360 http://www.waterfordcountryschool.org/programs/child-placing-services/ct-adoptions/
   2. Luke 12:6-7
   3. Psalm 139
   4. Acts 8:26-40
   5. Galations 5:25
   6. John 14:16, 26
   7. 1 Corinthians 12
   8. Galatians 5:22

Chapter 8: Gray Answers

1. Psalm 56:3
2. Philippians 4:13
3. John 3:16
4. Susan Warner; Anna Bartlett Warner (1860). Say and Seal. Lippincott & Company. pp. 115–116
5. 1 Kings 18:27-28
6. Genesis 9:20-21
7. Wikipedia. Wikimedia Foundation. Web. 10 Mar. 2016. <https://en.wikipedia.org/wiki/Religious_pluralism>.
8. John 16:11
9. Ephesians 6:10-17
10. James 2:17
11. http://www.worldvision.org/
12. Matthew 14:28-31
13. Matthew 11:2-3
14. Genesis 18:12
15. Matthew 26:39
16. Luke 10:38-42

ABOUT THE AUTHOR

Carrye Burr is an extrovert pastor's daughter who grew up and married an introvert architect, who happens to be very artistic. She's been writing for fun since she was a kid, and finally decided to step out in faith into her life-long dream of publishing a book. She's thankful that God is in the habit of using people who are weak, broken, and don't have it all together.

She and her husband, Jeff, live in CT with the three kids God has given them through birth and adoption. She is currently homeschooling her kids, but plans to take it a year at a time. She loves singing, slowly learning guitar, and enjoying quiet time with some coffee and friends.

Carrye has a passion to write and speak about the genuine struggles and joys of life and how to experience God tangibly. She hopes to inspire people to ask questions, be vulnerable, and realize we're not alone in our journeys. Follow her musings and add your voice to the conversation by visiting her blog:

www.lesstobemore.org

www.ingramcontent.com/pod-product-compliance
Lightning Source LLC
Chambersburg PA
CBHW032038040426
42449CB00007B/935